Cambridge Elements

Elements in Applied Social Psychology
edited by
Susan Clayton
College of Wooster, Ohio

UNDERSTANDING AND COPING IN SOCIAL RELATIONSHIPS WITH NARCISSISTS

Amy B. Brunell
The Ohio State University

Shaftesbury Road, Cambridge CB2 8EA, United Kingdom

One Liberty Plaza, 20th Floor, New York, NY 10006, USA

477 Williamstown Road, Port Melbourne, VIC 3207, Australia

314–321, 3rd Floor, Plot 3, Splendor Forum, Jasola District Centre, New Delhi – 110025, India

103 Penang Road, #05–06/07, Visioncrest Commercial, Singapore 238467

Cambridge University Press is part of Cambridge University Press & Assessment, a department of the University of Cambridge.

We share the University's mission to contribute to society through the pursuit of education, learning and research at the highest international levels of excellence.

www.cambridge.org
Information on this title: www.cambridge.org/9781009539692

DOI: 10.1017/9781108908306

When citing this work, please include a reference to the DOI 10.1017/9781108908306

First published 2024

A catalogue record for this publication is available from the British Library

ISBN 978-1-009-53969-2 Hardback
ISBN 978-1-108-82760-7 Paperback
ISSN 2631-777X (online)
ISSN 2631-7761 (print)

Understanding and Coping in Social Relationships with Narcissists

Elements in Applied Social Psychology

DOI: 10.1017/9781108908306
First published online: November 2024

Amy B. Brunell
The Ohio State University

Author for correspondence: Amy B. Brunell, brunell.2@osu.edu

Abstract: Narcissism is a trait that comes in different forms (agentic, communal, and vulnerable), which are all marked by characteristics such as entitlement, self-centeredness, and little empathy for others. One reason narcissism has gained attention among scholars and laypeople alike is because of its implications for social relationships. Narcissists' behaviors frequently have negative consequences for others. Whether their relationships are with coworkers or close relationship partners, interactions with narcissists can be challenging and emotionally taxing. Despite this, there is a sparse amount of research that addresses how to cope with difficult narcissistic relationships. This Element includes an overview of the trait forms of narcissism and discusses its implications for their social relationships. It provides a background about the development of narcissism and offers some research-informed suggestions for how to cope in narcissistic relationships. Future directions for research are also discussed.

Keywords: narcissism, social relationships, leadership, parenting, romantic relationships

ISBNs: 9781009539692 (HB), 9781108827607 (PB), 9781108908306 (OC)
ISSNs: 2631-777X (online), 2631-7761 (print)

Contents

1 Overview of the Origins of Narcissism

Narcissism is a complex variable as it refers to both a personality disorder and personality traits found in the normal population. Adding to this complexity is that narcissism as a personality dimension that comes in several forms. I begin by providing a brief overview of the origins of narcissism and explain the three forms it takes at the individual level. I then go on to discuss its implications for social relationships.

The concept of narcissism was derived from the Greek myth of Narcissus, a beautiful man who eschewed the love of others and treated those who fell in love with him with disdain and contempt. Nemesis, the goddess of retribution and revenge, decided to punish Narcissus for his behavior. She led him to a pool of water; when Narcissus saw his reflection in the water, he became transfixed with his own image and ultimately died rooted to the spot.

Early psychological thinking about narcissism included works by Sigmund Freud (1914/1991), who theorized that narcissism was a part of normal childhood development and was only pathological if it extended into adulthood. In other words, sometime during early childhood, parental and societal expectations teach the individual about the "right" ways to be in the social environment so that they aspire to attain an ideal sense of self. Clinical theories of narcissism were advanced by Austrian psychoanalysts Heinz Kohut (1971) and Otto Kernberg (1970; 1975), who each viewed narcissism as a defect in healthy development due to disturbances in early parental relationships. Narcissism was later codified in the Diagnostic and Statistical Manual, third edition (DSM III, American Psychiatric Association, 1980) as a personality disorder characterized by four primary characteristics:

(a) Grandiose sense of self-importance or uniqueness (e.g., exaggeration of achievements and talents, focus on the special nature of one's problem)
(b) Preoccupation with fantasies of unlimited success, power, brilliance, beauty, or ideal love
(c) Exhibitionism: The person requires constant attention and admiration
(d) Cool indifference or marked feelings of rage, inferiority, shame, humiliation, or emptiness in response to criticism, indifference to others, or defeat

Diagnosis also included at least two of the following characteristics:

(a) Entitlement: Expectation of special favors without assuming reciprocal responsibilities (e.g., surprise and anger that people will not do what is wanted)
(b) Interpersonal exploitativeness: Taking advantage of others to indulge own desires or for self-aggrandizement; disregard for the personal integrity and rights of others

(c) Relationships that characteristically alternate between the extremes of overidealization and devaluation
(d) Lack of empathy: Inability to recognize how others feel (e.g., unable to appreciate the distress of someone who is seriously ill).

The diagnostic criteria have been revised over time, but using the initial criteria for diagnosis gives the reader a sense of what people mean when they use the term "narcissism." Narcissistic Personality Disorder (NPD) is diagnosed through clinical evaluation and affects roughly 6 percent of the population (DSM-5; American Psychiatric Association, 2013). However, scholars have argued that these characteristics could also exist at less extreme levels in the normal population. Much of this research stemmed from the development and validation of the Narcissistic Personality Inventory (NPI) (Raskin & Hall, 1979; Raskin & Terry, 1988). The aim of this Element is to examine the multiple forms of narcissism found in the normal population. Given that narcissism is assessed on a continuum, everybody in the normal population falls somewhere on the continuum. For brevity's sake, when I refer to "narcissists," I am referring to those who score on the higher end of the continuum.

2 Trait Narcissism

In this section, I will explain several different forms of narcissism that have emerged in the research literature. I will then address how current theory has attempted to integrate these forms of narcissism.

2.1 Agentic Grandiose Narcissism

The agentic form of grandiose narcissism (called "agentic narcissism" from this point forward) is characterized by grandiosity, high self-esteem, extraversion, arrogance, and dominance (Miller & Campbell, 2008; Miller et al., 2017). Agentic narcissists have exalted self-views, especially on agentic traits such as competence and intelligence (Campbell, Rudich, & Sedikides, 2002). They believe themselves to be superior to others, even when these views conflict with reality (Grijalva & Zhang, 2016). For example, they believe themselves to be more attractive than others do and more intelligent than objective measures suggest (Gabriel et al., 1994). Relatedly, as a means of maintaining their sense of superiority, agentic narcissists derogate the characteristics of others, including their friends (Park & Colvin, 2015). They likewise desire to be admired by others (Campbell, 1999). They would prefer to have status than to have intimacy with others (Campbell, 1999).

When they are working with others, agentic narcissists will take credit for success and blame others for failure (Campbell et al., 2000). They work to procure short-term benefits for themselves, even when their decisions would cost themselves and others dearly in the future (Campbell et al., 2005).

One recent model of agentic narcissism that incorporates their need for admiration and their more antagonistic qualities is the Narcissistic Admiration and Rivalry Concept (NARC) (Back et al., 2013). The NARC differentiates these two central aspects of agentic narcissism. Narcissistic admiration reflects narcissists' agentic qualities and tendency to self-promote. The admiration dimension incorporates striving for uniqueness, grandiose fantasies, and charming behavior, which could lead to social power through popularity, social status, and attainment of social resources. Narcissistic rivalry, on the other hand, reflects agentic narcissists' antagonistic qualities, which come about when they feel socially threatened, such as when they receive negative feedback or social disapproval. In this case, agentic narcissists will use strategies to self-protect, such as devaluing others, aggression, or other means of tearing others down.

2.2 Communal Grandiose Narcissism

While grandiose narcissism concerns grandiosity, entitlement, and power, a growing amount of research has demonstrated that one can accomplish these motives not only in the agentic domain but in the communal domain as well. Communal narcissists seek out admiration by being caring and helpful (Gebauer et al., 2012). Although it seems on the surface that communal narcissists are deeply concerned with others, agentic motives are at the heart of their behavior (Gebauer & Sedikides, 2018). For example, in a study wherein participants were given personality feedback that empowered them, communal narcissists became *less* helpful in response (Giacomin & Jordan, 2015).

2.3 Vulnerable Narcissism

Vulnerable narcissism is characterized by low self-esteem and negative emotionality (e.g., Miller & Campbell, 2008), which includes increased anxiety and depression (Brunell & Buelow, 2019). Vulnerable narcissists tend to be socially inhibited, defensive, and vindictive (Hendin & Cheek, 1997). They are mistrusting of others and think that others' behaviors have malevolent intent (Wink, 1991). Perhaps because they are not very successful at regulating their self-esteem, they rely on external feedback from others (Besser & Priel, 2009). This makes vulnerable narcissists hypersensitive to social approval.

3 Theoretical Models

Although these three forms of narcissism manifest themselves differently, what they have in common are the core characteristics of entitlement, self-centeredness, and a lack of empathy for others (Hansen-Brown, 2018). There are a growing number of theoretical models being developed to bridge multiple forms of narcissism under the umbrella of "narcissism" for increased conceptual clarity.

Two models that have produced momentum in understanding narcissism more broadly are the Narcissism Spectrum Model (Krizan & Herlache, 2018) and the Trifurcate Model (Crowe et al., 2019). According to the Narcissism Spectrum Model, a defining feature of narcissism is entitled self-importance, which is shared by both agentic and vulnerable narcissists. Entitled self-importance incorporates egotism combined with a sense of entitlement and a belief that one is deserving of special treatment (Krizan & Herlach, 2018). Agentic narcissism combines entitled self-importance with being bold and approach-oriented, whereas vulnerable narcissism combines entitled self-importance with being oversensitive and avoidant. In a similar vein, the Trifurcate Model defines narcissism as consisting of three parts: agentic extraversion, self-centered antagonism, and narcissistic neuroticism. Self-centered antagonism incorporates egotism, a sense of entitlement, and noncompliance (Miller & Campbell, 2008; Miller et al., 2017). Agentic narcissism combines agentic extraversion and self-centered antagonism, whereas vulnerable narcissism combines self-centered antagonism with narcissistic neuroticism. Thus, both models indicate that egotism and entitlement form a narcissistic core.

These two models have served as significant theoretical advances to our understanding of agentic and vulnerable narcissism. However, they did not incorporate other relevant constructs, such as communal narcissism, which have been incorporated into the Circumplex of Personality Metatraits (Rogoza et al., 2019). Both agentic and vulnerable narcissism were found in the radius associated with disinhibition, which reflects antagonism (Rogoza et al., 2019; Strus & Cieciuch, 2017). Agentic narcissism fit closest in the region combining antagonism with sensation-seeking, whereas vulnerable fit closest to the region associated with disharmony. Communal narcissism fit closest to the region associated with integration because communal narcissism combines grandiosity with prosocial attitudes toward others.

4 Gender and Age Differences in Trait Narcissism

As far back as the 1970s and 1980s, social critic Peter Slater (1974) suggested that narcissism was a trait that favored men because they invest their time and energy in narcissistic pursuits by focusing on achievement, power, and status. Another scholar (Philipson, 1985) noted that narcissism, and specifically diagnoses of NPD, was substantially higher among men than women. Basing her arguments on psychoanalyst Margaret Mahler's (1963) work on separation–individuation theory, she theorized that disruptions in the process of individuating and separating from the mother during infancy and early childhood would affect boys differently than girls. In the process of separation, boys are provided more physical and psychological freedom and independence than girls are. When mothers are inconsistent in their empathy toward their sons, boys become extremely self-centered and grandiose in order to maintain their ego boundaries from her. At the same time, mothers' inconsistent empathy creates failures in boys to internalize positive self-images, leaving them with the need for outside approval to maintain feelings of self-worth. Given that girls are the same sex as their mothers, they are afforded less opportunities for separation from their mothers because they are more likely to be seen by the mother as extensions of the self. Girls are also more likely to define themselves in relation to others and identify with their mothers. Thus, disruptions in maternal empathy for girls is more likely to result in a lack of autonomy and greater dependency on others. For these reasons, Philipson argued that narcissism was more likely to be manifested in men than women.

Soon afterward, scholars began to empirically research the claim that men, on average, were more narcissistic than women. Watson et al. (1987) examined gender differences in a measure of agentic narcissism and a measure of NPD. They found that men scored higher on agentic narcissism than women, and specifically on the subfacets of exploitativeness and superiority. However, there were no gender differences on the measure of NPD. Since then, plenty of research studies have replicated the finding that men are more agentic narcissistic than women (e.g., Tschanz et al., 1998), but plenty of studies have not (e.g., Bleske-Rechek et al., 2008).

In an effort to systematically review the magnitude of gender differences in narcissism, Grijalva et al. (2015) completed a comprehensive meta-analysis. In contrast to the psychoanalytic perspective or using an evolutionary psychology perspective, an essentialist perspective that emphasizes men's dominance in the access to mates (e.g. Ainsworth & Maner, 2012), Grijalva et al. (2015) used Wood and Eagly's (2012) biosocial construction model to support their claims. In the biosocial construction model, they argue that biological differences in men and women (such as physical size and strength) created a gendered division of labor, with women taking care of the children and the home and men garnering economic resources, such as money and food. Because we observe men and women doing different tasks, we infer different dispositional qualities among men (e.g., competence) and women (e.g., nurturing). This process, in turn, produces beliefs and expectations about gender, which we internalize during the socialization process in childhood. Agentic qualities, such as dominant, assertive, and competitive, become associated with men and communal qualities, such as, caring, sympathetic, and helpful, become associated with women. According to Rudman (1998), not only are the content of gender stereotypes such that men are agentic and women are communal, men and women also feel the pressure to behave in gender-stereotypic ways.

Given that agentic narcissism is associated with high agentic qualities and low communal qualities (Brunell & Campbell, 2011; Campbell et al., 2006), it was therefore expected that men would be more agentic narcissistic than women. In addition, given gender stereotypes, women would be expected to suppress the agentic displays associated with narcissism (Grijalva et al., 2015). In their meta-analysis, Grijalva and colleagues examined 355 studies that included almost 471,000 participants, most of whom had completed the NPI. They found that there was a small effect (d = .26) that men were more agentic narcissistic than women across these studies, and this effect appears to be driven by the NPI facets of exploitativeness/entitlement and leadership/authority (based on the factor structure reported by Ackerman et al., 2011). This difference remained stable over time and across different age groups. Follow-up work replicated the finding that men are higher in agentic narcissism across a variety of measures that purport to assess agentic narcissism and concurred that gender differences are stable across the adult lifespan (Weidman et al., 2023).

Although there is significantly less research examining vulnerable narcissism, Grijalva and colleagues (2015) also examined potential gender differences in vulnerable narcissism. Men and women did not reliably differ on vulnerable narcissism. However, additional research found gender differences (or not) depending on which measure of vulnerable narcissism was used. One commonly used measure of vulnerable narcissism is the Hypersensitive Narcissism Scale (HSNS) (Hendin & Cheek, 1997). Research has found that men scored higher on the HSNS than women (Chan & Cheung, 2022; Weidman et al., 2023). Other scholars have recently proposed that the HSNS has a two-factor structure, with one factor containing items pertaining to self-centeredness and the other pertaining to rejection sensitivity (Stone & Bartholomay, 2022). When these factors were taken into consideration, men scored higher on the facet of self-centeredness, but women scored higher on the rejection sensitivity facet. Another measure of narcissism, the brief Pathological Narcissism Inventory (Schoenleber et al., 2015), contains a facet measuring vulnerable narcissism. Gender differences in vulnerable narcissism on this measure were not reliable (Weidman et al., 2023). Communal narcissism was not examined in any of these papers.

Additional research examining gender differences in empathy and narcissism utilized the Narcissism Spectrum Scale (Malkin, 2015), which is a measure of narcissism that is used in clinical practice and combines aspects of grandiose and vulnerable narcissism (Chukwuorji et al., 2020). They sought to examine gender differences in narcissism among university students in Nigeria, specifically addressing whether the correlation between narcissism and empathy is different for men and women. They used a multifaceted measure of empathy (Interpersonal Reactivity Index, Davis, 1980), which includes four dimensions: fantasy (identifying with characters in fictional situations such as movies and novels), perspective-taking (taking another's point of view), empathic concern (having compassion and concern for others), and personal distress (experiencing feelings of anxiety and discomfort resulting from observing others' negative experiences. As expected, they found that men were more narcissistic than women and that narcissism correlated with lower empathy across all dimensions. Looking at each dimension specifically, for men, narcissism was associated with lower personal distress and not significantly correlated with any other dimension of empathy. For women, narcissism was negatively correlated with all four dimensions of empathy.

In addition to examining gender differences in narcissism, many scholars have also been interested in whether narcissism changes across the lifespan. Research on narcissism and age began with cross-sectional data that showed a negative correlation between age and agentic narcissism (e.g., Foster et al., 2003; Hill & Roberts, 2012; Wilson & Sibley, 2011). This finding has been extended to include measures of vulnerable narcissism as well (Weidman et al., 2023). Weidman et al. proposed that declines in narcissism with age might come about as people mature and experience important life changes in their social roles. Furthermore, with age, people also experience failures, setbacks, and challenges that might explain a marked decrease in narcissism (Foster et al., 2003). Research has yet to examine age differences in communal narcissism.

Cross-sectional data suggest that there are changes in narcissism over time, but longitudinal data are needed to support this claim. Longitudinal studies likewise suggest that people become less narcissistic with age, but also highlight the nuance that occurs across different developmental stages. Carlson and Gjerde's (2009) research found that agentic narcissism increases between the ages of fourteen and eighteen and then stabilizes into emerging adulthood. Additional research further suggests that agentic narcissism may be stable during emerging adulthood (Grosz et al., 2019). When examining the period of time between young adulthood and midlife, agentic narcissism decreases (Wetzel et al., 2020). Furthermore, when using multiple samples of longitudinal data for participants from the ages of thirteen to seventy-seven (born between

1923 and 1969), measures of agentic narcissism and vulnerable narcissism decrease across the lifespan (Chopik & Grimm, 2019). No longitudinal research has investigated communal narcissism.

Some have argued that there are cohort or generational differences (Chopik & Grimm, 2019; Twenge et al., 2008a; 2008b), but this is hotly disputed (Donnellan et al., 2009; Trzesniewski et al., 2008). Adding to the confusion about this topic is that some scholars point out that data suggest that later-born birth cohorts are lower in narcissism (Chopik & Grimm, 2019), while other scholars argue that later-born birth cohorts are higher in narcissism (Twenge et al., 2008a; 2008b). It should be noted, however, that different measures of narcissism have been evaluated in the quest to answer this question. The Grijalva et al. (2015) meta-analysis examined this question and found no evidence for cohort differences in their study, but more data are needed to examine differences in vulnerable and communal narcissism as most data relied on measures of agentic narcissism.

5 Trait Narcissism's Relations to Other Personality Models

5.1 Connections to the Five-Factor Model and the Big Five

The theoretical advances in the investigation of narcissism have highlighted the extent to which narcissism is associated with variables in the Five-Factor Model or Big Five variables. Understanding the personality correlates of narcissism is challenging because it depends not only on how narcissism is measured but also in how personality is measured. The Five-Factor Model and the Big Five, for example, appear to be similar but come from different origins and therefore have slightly different content (Visser, 2018). The newer HEXACO model of personality introduces a six-factor framework and has accounted for variance not captured by the Five-Factor Model or Big Five (Lee & Ashton, 2012; Lee et al., 2013). Rather than getting into the weeds on the differences in measures, I take a broad stroke view of how narcissism variables appear to map onto broader personality assessments.

Generally, agentic narcissism measures tend to be associated with low neuroticism and agreeableness and high extraversion (Miller & Campbell, 2008; Trull & McCrae, 2002). Extraversion is associated with gregariousness, liveliness, boldness, positive affect, and is therefore associated with better life satisfaction (Lee et al., 2008) and positive health outcomes (Nettle, 2005). Neuroticism is associated with negative emotions, anxiety, and depression (Lahey, 2009), which suggests that agentic narcissists do not experience a lot of personal distress. Agreeableness as measured by the Five-Factor Model and the Big Five Personality perspectives are correlated, but the Five-Factor Model appears to be better at accounting for agentic narcissism because its facets contain measures of modesty and straightforwardness, whereas the Big Five perspective focuses more on being helpful, forgiving, and trusting (Miller et al., 2011; Visser, 2018). The HEXACO model contains considerable overlap with Five-Factor Models and the Big Five (Visser, 2018). Emotionality contains the anxiety component of neuroticism, whereas the agreeableness facet contains more of the anger/hostility aspects. Honesty-humility concerns fairness, sincerity, greed avoidance, and modesty. The straightforwardness and modesty aspects of agreeableness in the Five-Factor Model is encompassed by the honesty-humility facet to demonstrate that agentic narcissism has a higher correlation with agreeableness. In this view, agentic narcissism correlates with extraversion and honesty-humility (Lee & Ashton, 2005), suggesting that low honesty-humility and high extraversion appear to be the key ingredients of agentic narcissism (Lee & Ashton, 2012).

Only one study has examined the personality correlates of communal narcissism. This study (Rogoza & Fatfouta, 2019) found that communal narcissism was associated with lower neuroticism, higher extraversion, higher openness to experience, higher agreeableness, and higher conscientiousness. These findings provide some evidence that communal narcissists are high functioning.

With regard to vulnerable narcissism, there is a growing amount of research suggesting that vulnerable narcissism is associated with high neuroticism and possibly low extraversion. From a Five-Factor Model perspective, because vulnerable narcissists tend not to be trusting, they are lower in agreeableness. Thus, agentic and vulnerable narcissism are both associated with lower agreeableness, but for different reasons (Miller et al., 2011). Similar patterns for vulnerable narcissism have also been found from a Big Five perspective (Thomas et al., 2012). Most of the variance in vulnerable narcissism is accounted for by neuroticism followed by antagonism (Miller et al., 2018). Thus, it seems that vulnerable narcissists are disagreeable because of affective dysregulation and distrust, whereas agentic narcissists are disagreeable for instrumental reasons like personal gain.

In summary, both agentic and communal narcissists score low on neuroticism and high on extraversion. Where they diverge is in how agreeable they are. Agentic narcissists are more disagreeable, but communal narcissists, who view themselves as being exceptionally helpful (Gebauer et al., 2012), score high on agreeableness. Given that vulnerable narcissists tend to experience negative emotionality (Miller & Campbell, 2008), are hypersensitive (Hendin & Cheek, 1997), and mistrusting of others (Wink, 1991), they tend to score higher on neuroticism and lower on agreeableness.

5.2 Connection to the Dark Personality Traits

In the literature, narcissism is frequently considered in conjunction with other dark personality traits, most notably subclinical psychopathy and Machiavellianism. Together, they are referred to as "the Dark Triad" (Paulhus & Williams, 2002). In the context of the Dark Triad, narcissism refers to the agentic form of narcissism (communal narcissism has not been studied). Psychopathy reflects a callous and impulsive nature; a person high in psychopathy lacks empathy for others, is self-centered and inattentive, and lacks self-control (Salekin & Lynam, 2010). People who score higher on Machiavellianism tend to be emotionally detached, manipulative, exploitative, and cynical (Furnham et al., 2013; Rauthmann & Will, 2011). There tends to be a moderate correlation between agentic narcissism and psychopathy and a small correlation between agentic narcissism and Machiavellianism (Paulhus & Williams, 2002; Turner & Webster, 2018). Very often, agentic narcissism, psychopathy, and Machiavellianism are used as independent predictors of dark behavior. For example, it appears that when it comes to aggressive responding, agentic narcissism is associated with aggression in response to ego threat and psychopathy in response to physical threat, while Machiavellianism is not associated with either one (Jones & Paulhus, 2010).

Recently, research has begun to determine the extent to which vulnerable narcissism is associated with the Dark Triad traits. There appears to be a small to medium correlation between vulnerable narcissism and Machiavellianism, and little to no association with psychopathy (Breeden et al., 2020; Kajonius & Bjorkman, 2020; March et al., 2020; Pilch, 2020). However, Miller and colleagues (Miller et al., 2010) proposed a Vulnerable Dark Triad that consists of vulnerable narcissism, a subscale of psychopathy, and borderline personality disorder. The subscale of psychopathy reflects social deviance and centers around behavior problems and impulsivity (Lynam & Derefinko, 2006). This dimension of psychopathy consists of an antagonistic personality style, disinhibition, and negative emotionality. People who score higher on measures of bipolar personality disorder are more neurotic, impulsive, and interpersonally antagonistic (Samuel & Widiger, 2008). The three dimensions of the Vulnerable Dark Triad have high neuroticism, disagreeableness, and increased psychological distress and dysfunction in common. To test how the Dark Triad and the Vulnerable Dark Triad differentially predict behavior, Edwards and colleagues (2017) examined criminal behavior among adult offenders. They found that the Dark Triad and the Vulnerable Dark Triad were both associated with crimes, but in different ways. The Dark Triad and the Vulnerable Dark Triad both accounted for fraud. However, only the Vulnerable Dark Triad accounted for robbery and theft, and only the Dark Triad predicted crimes against persons, such as assault. The Dark Triad accounted for the obstruction of justice, such as committing perjury, while the Vulnerable Dark Triad predicted drug offenses.

Additional research has begun to examine narcissism in the context of additional dark personality traits, such as spite, greed, and sadism. The entitlement/exploitative features of agentic narcissism appear to be modestly correlated with spite as does a measure of vulnerable narcissism (Marcus et al., 2014). Greed appears to be moderately associated with trait narcissism, but it is more strongly associated with psychopathy and Machiavellianism (Veselka et al., 2014).

The investigation of sadism appears to have received the most traction in the investigation of a Dark Tetrad. Sadism might be considered multidimensional; for example, verbal sadism (humiliating and mocking others), physical sadism (desire for subjugation and enjoyment of hurting others), and vicarious sadism (gaining pleasure through observing or fantasizing about violence) (Johnson et al., 2019). Agentic narcissism has small to moderate correlations with all three dimensions of sadism (Johnson et al., 2019). One aspect all dimensions have in common is emotional callousness (Lee, 2019); even so, each dimension of the Dark Tetrad might predict different motives or outcomes. For example, when it comes to aggression, sadists aggress for enjoyment's sake (Buckels et al., 2013), whereas agentic narcissistic aggression centers on responses to ego threat (Jones & Paulhus, 2010). In an investigation on how people respond to discussions with others who are mourning the loss of a loved one, sadists said the mourners were funny, their pain enjoyable, and felt that the mourner owed them for investing their time and effort in listening to them (Lee, 2019). Those who scored higher in psychopathy reported more schadenfreude, while those who scored higher in Machiavellianism reported feeling annoyed by the conversation because there was nothing to be gained from it personally. Perhaps surprisingly, agentic narcissists reported feeling less annoyed by the conversation, suggesting that agentic narcissists demonstrate empathy when such displays are needed (Vonk et al., 2013).

Taken together, both forms of narcissism are a part of a collection of traits that predict dark behavior, including aggression, dishonesty, and emotional callousness. The dark qualities of narcissism – whether the grandiose forms or the vulnerable form – suggest difficulties in their interpersonal functioning. In the sections that follow, I highlight research demonstrating how narcissists behave in the workplace and in their romantic relationships. Most of the research in these domains have investigated agentic narcissism, but I include research on vulnerable narcissism and communal narcissism when possible.

6 Trait Narcissism in the Workplace

6.1 Agentic Narcissism and Civility

One form of deviant workplace behavior is incivility, which reflects an ambiguous intention to harm somebody in violation of norms of mutual respect (Lata & Chaudhary, 2020). There are consequences for targets of incivility at both the personal and organizational level. For example, at the personal level, incivility can adversely affect workers' performance, job satisfaction, and psychological well-being (Schilpzand et al., 2016). From an organizational standpoint, collectively, there are lower productivity and performance (Porath & Erez, 2007). A recent study showed that especially in environments that are largely supportive and create a sense of community, agentic narcissists are more uncivil toward their peers, possibly because their "true colors" emerge in situations where there are no power differentials (Lata & Chaudhary, 2020).

One defining characteristic of agentic narcissism is the tendency to self-enhance because they desire to see themselves in overly positive ways and to have others view them in an extremely positive fashion (Morf & Rhodewalt, 2001). Given this desire, agentic narcissists do not take kindly to incidents of incivility in the workplace because they attempt to avoid threatening treatment and strive to protect themselves (Chen et al., 2013). That is, being targets of incivility means there is a discrepancy between how agentic narcissists are treated and how they think they ought to be treated. Therefore, when there is incivility – or even a lack of praise – in the workplace, agentic narcissistic workers tend to disengage from their work (Chen et al., 2013; Morf et al., 2000) because disengagement allows them to reduce exposure to hostile others at work and minimize the extent to which they invest their sense of self in their work environment. Consequently, agentic narcissistic employees who feel they have been targets of incivility also have lower task performance (Chen et al., 2013).

6.2 Agentic Narcissism and Counterproductive Work Behavior

A common thread for agentic narcissism in the workplace is the engagement in counterproductive work behaviors, which include behaviors such as workplace incivility, bullying, aggression, and even embezzlement and other white-collar crimes (Bogart et al., 2004; Penney & Spector, 2002). Two meta-analyses examined the extent to which agentic narcissism was associated with counterproductive work behavior, and both studies revealed large effect sizes. However, as ingroup collectivism increased, agentic narcissists engaged in less counterproductive work behaviors (Grijalva & Newman, 2015; O'Boyle et al., 2011). That is, work cultures that value loyalty to organizations and group cohesiveness among team members tend to have fewer incidents of counterproductive work behavior (House et al., 2004). These cultures are less tolerant of agentic narcissistic behaviors such as self-promotion (because it is interpreted as a violation of group norms), violations to the norm of social exchange, and manipulation (Van Dyne et al., 2000). Additional analyses have revealed that counterproductive work behaviors tend to be driven by the entitlement/exploitativeness facet of agentic narcissism and tempered by the leadership/authority facet (Grijalva & Newman, 2015).

6.3 Agentic Narcissism, Leadership, and Followership

Poor leadership is one of the most influential predictors of employee cynicism (Bommer et al., 2005). Agentic narcissists are likely to fall under the category of poor leadership, despite the tendency for them to emerge as leaders (Brunell et al., 2008; Grijalva et al., 2015; Nevicka et al., 2011) and to occupy positions of power such as presidents and CEOs (Chatterjee & Hambrick, 2007). Because agentic narcissistic leaders (a) have leadership visions that are self-serving rather than serving the teams they lead (Conger, 1997), (b) self-promote to gain recognition (Rosenthal & Pittinsky, 2006), and (c) use strategies of deception, manipulation, and intimidation to get their way (Glad, 2002), they foster organizational cynicism. Organizational cynicism refers to a negative attitude toward one's organization, such as beliefs that the organization lacks integrity as well as behavior such as disparaging the organization (Dean et al., 1998). In a study of university hospital nurses in Turkey, the association between leaders' agentic narcissism and organizational cynicism was mediated by employee psychological strain, such as feelings of anxiety, depression, exhaustion, and loss of self-confidence (Erkutlu & Chafra, 2017).

If agentic narcissistic coworkers are "emotional vampires" in the workplace, how do they rise to leadership roles so often? One theory suggests that there is considerable overlap between agentic narcissistic characteristics and how people think leaders "should be" (Nevicka, 2018). This helps with agentic narcissists' ability to rise through the ranks. Furthermore, their charm, enthusiasm, dominance, and confidence tend to assist them in making positive first impressions on people (Back et al., 2010), even though these positive impressions do not last (e.g., Paulhus, 1998). Second, agentic narcissists desire to lead and rate themselves positively on leadership (Brunell et al., 2008; Grijalva et al., 2015; Judge et al., 2006). Therefore, they actively seek out opportunities to climb the corporate ladder (Zitek & Jordan, 2016).

One question concerns how effective agentic narcissistic leaders are. On the one hand, agentic narcissistic leaders are innovative (Gerstner et al., 2013), charismatic, and impart bold visions to followers (Galvin et al., 2010). They are decisive and persistent (Wallace et al., 2009). When faced with criticism, agentic narcissists are more willing to do tasks that would enable them to prove themselves (Nevicka et al., 2016). Furthermore, during difficult and uncertain times, their followers find their leadership to be reassuring (Nevicka et al., 2013). One study demonstrated that agentic narcissism among US presidents was associated with better crisis management, public persuasiveness, and the ability to push through an agenda and initiate legislation (Watts et al., 2013).

On the other hand, agentic narcissists have a host of negative traits, such as overconfidence and self-serving behavior, impulsivity, entitlement, and a sense of superiority, which can have negative consequences for an organization (Judge et al., 2009). They disregard advice from others (Kausel et al., 2015) because they believe their ideas are the best (Maccoby, 2000). While they are decisive, they also make risky and volatile decisions (Chatterjee & Hambrick, 2007). Agentic narcissistic leaders have a habit of dominating discussions and are poor at sharing information with subordinates, which in turn leads to reduced team performance (Nevicka et al., 2011). Thus, there could be considerable negative consequences from agentic narcissistic leadership.

However, whether or not agentic narcissistic leaders are effective depends, in part, on what is studied and how it is studied. For example, one study examined the extent to which agentic narcissism among major league baseball team owners was associated with team performance (Resick et al., 2009). This study found that team owners' agentic narcissism was associated with lower contingent reward leadership, which refers to recognizing and rewarding performance such as through pay increases and promotion for when organization objectives are met. This contingent reward leadership, in turn, predicted less external influence (building relationships with important constituents such as customers or donors), but was also associated with lower manager turnover, suggesting that the managers wind up feeling empowered. Importantly, however, is that the owner's agentic narcissism was not associated with the team's performance.

Yet there are times when leader agentic narcissism has consequences for subordinates, such as their job engagement or job performance. Agentic narcissists thrive on recognition and positive attention from others (DuBrin, 2012). One effective way to gain this kind of attention is to obtain good results, which can be accomplished by motivating and guiding followers as well as keeping more negative reactions to them at bay (Campbell et al., 2011). Furthermore, when leaders give followers respect and bestow trust onto them (Robbins & Judge, 2011), good relationships are developed. One study found that positive exchanges between leaders and followers mediated the association between leader agentic narcissism and efforts made by the team to improve team performance (Ha et al., 2020). These exchanges were more likely to occur when followers perceived that they were treated fairly by the leader and the organization (Ha et al., 2020).

Furthermore, it is important to note that leaders themselves have numerous qualities (Owens et al., 2015). It may seem counterintuitive, but there is research demonstrating that even agentic narcissists can display high levels of humility (such as by acknowledging one does not know the answer to a problem) (Ou et al., 2014; Owens et al., 2015). When agentic narcissistic leaders demonstrate higher levels of humility, they can be viewed as effective because their acts of humility temper their more noxious agentic narcissistic qualities.

Another direction to explore with regard to followership is when the follower is narcissistic (Benson & Jordan, 2018). Agentic narcissists have a tendency to be dissatisfied with their role as follower because they believe the position of follower is not a reflection of their true abilities (Benson et al., 2016). They are harder to mentor (Allen et al., 2009) because they are less likely to take advice (Kausel et al., 2015). When they are in roles as followers, they tend to be less motivated because they see themselves as leaders and prefer to be leaders (Arthur et al., 2011). For this reason, they prefer hierarchy in an organization when they can see themselves moving up the corporate ladder and dislike hierarchy when they do not perceive a means to advance (Benson & Jordan, 2018; Zitek & Jordan, 2016). In this situation, they are likely to move on to another position.

6.4 Communal Narcissism in the Workplace

To the best of my knowledge, research has not yet examined how communal narcissists behave in the workplace. One study has examined the kind of jobs that communal narcissists might be attracted to. This study found that communal narcissists are more attracted to companies that describe themselves in agentic ways ("dynamic company," "results-oriented," seeking employees who are "assertive, performance-oriented and goal-oriented") than communal ways ("trusted company," "cooperative," and seeking employees who are "considerate, polite, and dependable") (Fatfouta, 2021). One reason might be that agentic work environments validate communal narcissists more than communal work environments do. Recall that communal narcissists seek to find means of validating their sense of power (Gebauer et al., 2012; Giacomin & Jordan, 2015).

From this, we can speculate how communal narcissists might behave in the workplace. They might be less inclined to be uncivil or engage in workplace bullying behaviors because they want to be seen as "the best" at making the company a better place to work. There is a good likelihood that they see themselves as good leaders and would desire leadership roles. However, much like their agentic grandiose narcissistic counterparts, they are likely to think they are better leaders and better team players than they actually are.

6.5 Vulnerable Narcissism in the Workplace

Surprisingly, little research has examined vulnerable narcissism in the workplace. One noteworthy exception was a recent study (Wirtz & Rigotti, 2020) that examined the extent to which supervisor agentic narcissism and subordinate vulnerable narcissism combine to predict work engagement. These authors examined 71 leaders and their 235 team members. They found that vulnerable narcissism was negatively associated with work engagement, and it was moderated by leaders' agentic narcissism, such that at higher levels of leader agentic narcissism, vulnerable narcissists declined in work engagement. This could be because vulnerable narcissists, who already feel poorly about themselves, are less inclined to engage in their work when they are met with potential abusive supervision or derogatory behavior from their supervisor.

Taken together, the research suggest that working with narcissists, especially agentic narcissists, creates difficulties in the workplace. First, both agentic and vulnerable narcissists disengage from their work when they feel threatened or their egos are bruised. Agentic narcissists can also behave in uncivil ways, engage in destructive behaviors at work, and are poor at communicating with their team. Such behaviors have consequences not only for the individual but also for the team and even the organization.

7 Narcissus in Romantic Relationships

The bulk of the research on close relationships has investigated the agentic form of narcissism. However, research has begun to examine the other forms of narcissism as well. In this section, I summarize what is known about all three forms of narcissism.

7.1 Agentic Narcissism in Romantic Relationships

The primary goal of agentic narcissists is to gain admiration from their partners and status by association (such as by having a trophy partner) (Campbell, 1999). Communal goals such as fostering intimacy, care, and concern are not nearly as important to agentic narcissists as are their concerns about status and admiration. For example, in one study, participants wrote about what matters to them in relationships (Campbell, 1999). Agentic narcissists were more likely to mention admiration and status and less likely to mention caring in their responses. Across several additional studies, agentic narcissists were likely to indicate feeling more attraction for a partner who admires them rather than one who cares about them (Campbell, 1999). This pattern was first investigated in the United States but has been replicated in a collectivistic culture (i.e., Thailand) as well (Tanchotsrinon et al., 2007).

This pattern of valuing status and power over care and intimacy extends to agentic narcissists' sexual relationships. In the bedroom, agentic narcissists are more interested in power and personal pleasure than they are about closeness and love (Foster et al., 2006). Their goal is to have casual sexual experiences and more sexual conquests (Schmitt et al., 2017). When in long-term relationships, their primary motives for sex appear to be self-affirmation (e.g., affirming one's sexual attractiveness) and to restore positive mood (Gewirtz-Meydan et al., 2017). Furthermore, women's agentic narcissism was associated with lower intimacy motivation among their partners, perhaps because intimacy in heterosexual relationships is typically driven by women and warmth and intimacy are lacking among agentic narcissistic women.

When agentic narcissists are in dating relationships, they keep their partners guessing about their interest in the relationship and treat dating as a game (Campbell, Foster, & Finkel, 2002; Rohmann et al., 2012). Why do agentic narcissists play games? In their quest for status, power, and independence, game playing enables agentic narcissists to maintain their power and freedom through the principle of least interest (Campbell, Foster, & Finkel 2002), which is the idea that the person who is less invested in the relationship has more power in the relationship (Sprecher et al., 2006; Waller, 1938). In addition, they delight in inducing jealousy to maintain power and control in their partnerships (Tortoriello et al., 2017). Thus, although long-term relationships come with the benefits of emotional intimacy and social support, agentic narcissists simply do not seem to find emotional intimacy and social support to be beneficial (Campbell, 1999). For this reason, agentic narcissists may not be particularly motivated to establish long-term relationships.

Relatedly, agentic narcissists lack commitment in their relationships. Research using the Investment Model has shown that there are three main factors for maintaining long-lasting relationships (Rusbult, 1980; 1983). The first is relationship satisfaction. The second is one's perceptions of alternatives to the relationship one is in, which includes partnering with someone else or preferring to be single. The more high-quality alternatives a person has to the current relationship, the less likely they are to stay in the relationship. Lastly, the extent to which people feel invested in a relationship, the more likely they are to commit to the relationship. Investments include shared resources, friends, and children, for example. For agentic narcissists, because they are chronically looking for a better "trophy" partner, their perceptions of having more (high quality) alternatives predict lower relationship commitment (Campbell & Foster, 2002).

So why do people get involved with agentic narcissists? It seems that in the short-term agentic narcissists tend to be deemed attractive, confident, charming, likeable, and fun (Brunell & Campbell, 2011). They have mate-appeal (Jauk et al., 2016) and other qualities that draw others in (Back et al., 2010). In addition, it is not uncommon that agentic narcissists are attracted to other agentic narcissists (Grosz et al., 2015) as they share common goals for the relationship.

In one study, college students were asked to compare previous relationships they had with someone who was an agentic narcissist and someone who was not (Brunell & Campbell, 2011). First, they wrote their narratives about each relationship and then answered some additional questions. Their stories were then coded for themes. The good parts about dating agentic narcissists were that they were ambitious, popular, charming, and sexually attractive. The worst parts of the relationship were that they were deceptive, controlling, materialistic, and made their partners feel like a trophy. Participants also believed their agentic narcissistic partners were less committed and faithful to them. When asked about their relationship satisfaction over the course of the relationship with both kinds of partners, there was a steep decline in satisfaction in relationships with agentic narcissists as their more insufferable qualities became more apparent. Interestingly, the participants were not particularly unhappy at the end of the relationship with the nonnarcissist. They reported that they grew apart, were not compatible, or regretted that this relationship ended.

Although much research has indicated that agentic narcissists seem to be less interested in forming long-term relationships, many ultimately do form them, nonetheless. In the past few years, more research has focused on ongoing relationships with agentic narcissists, rather than on shorter relationships among adolescents and young adults. For example, studies have been done that observe couples having a conversation in the lab (Lamkin et al., 2017; Peterson & DeHart, 2014). The data from these studies suggest that relationships with agentic narcissists become increasingly more dissatisfying for both the narcissist and the partner over time (Lavner et al., 2016; Ye et al., 2016).

One reason partners of agentic narcissists might become less happy over time is that agentic narcissistic partners seem to miss how their noxious behavior impacts their partners (Foster & Brunell, 2018). For example, they engage in frequent angry and hostile communication (Lamkin et al., 2017; Peterson & DeHart, 2014). They have extreme negative reactions to criticism, rejection, and failure. Even when agentic narcissists have minor disagreements with their partners, they report feeling less committed to their relationship even after the conflict is over. This pattern extends to minor disagreements about hypothetical situations such as where they would like to take a dream vacation. Furthermore, they purposely make their partners feel insecure and jealous as a means to maintain power and control in the relationship (Tortoriello et al., 2017). In addition, agentic narcissists experience elevated jealousy themselves when they are in relationships (Chin et al., 2017), possibly because they use their own behavior to judge what they expect of others. However, their own jealousy might come about from experiences with having their romantic partners stolen away from them (Kardum et al., 2015).

Lastly, research has suggested that agentic narcissists are more likely to engage in sexual coercion and intimate partner violence. For example, both agentic narcissistic men and women indicate a tendency to use an arsenal of strategies when their partners have rebuffed their sexual advances. These include persistence (such as kissing the person), manipulation, exploitation (such as getting their partner drunk), and use of physical threats or force (Blinkhorn et al., 2015). Furthermore, both agentic narcissistic men and women tend to be more accepting of intimate partner violence (Blinkhorn et al., 2016).

7.2 Communal Narcissism in Relationships

Little research has investigated how communal narcissists behave in their relationships. In a preliminary study, we found that communal narcissists reported more positive perceptions of their relationship behaviors and relationship quality (Drotleff & Brunell, 2020). We also investigated how communal narcissists would perceive their relationships when they were empowered versus when they were disempowered (Drotleff & Brunell, 2020). The inspiration of this study initially came from research examining how helpful communal narcissists were when they felt empowered, with results highlighting that communal narcissists became less helpful when they were empowered (Giacomin & Jordan, 2015). Given that interpersonal relationships are at the heart of self-enhancement on communal traits, in our study, we hypothesized that when communal narcissists felt empowered, it would alter their motivations about their relationships, such as the intention to engage in infidelity. Research has shown that having elevated power is linked to increased infidelity (Lammers et al., 2011) as is agentic narcissism (Altınok & Kılıç, 2020). Furthermore, agentic narcissism has been associated with perceiving higher power in relationships more generally (Vrabel et al., 2020). Thus, it was possible that like their agentic counterparts, empowered communal narcissists would indicate greater intentions to cheat. On the other hand, evidence has suggested that people cheat when they perceive a lack of power in their relationships (Prins et al., 1993). Thus, it was possible to find that communal narcissists who were led to feel less empowered might have been more likely to engage in infidelity even though being a good relationship partner seems to be at the center of a communal narcissists' self-enhancement bias.

In our study, we recruited 208 participants who indicated they were in "exclusive" relationships from a research participant pool. As part of a larger packet of personality questionnaires, they were asked to complete the Communal Narcissism Inventory (Gebauer et al., 2012). The other questionnaires were simply used as a cover for the power manipulation. Participants were given false feedback about how powerful they would be later in life by using the same power manipulation as Giacomin and Jordan (2015). In the low-power feedback condition, participants were told that they "will not be in a position of power later in life," whereas those in the high-power condition were told they "will be in a position of power later in life." Following the manipulation, participants were asked questions about their relationships that included the Intentions toward Infidelity Scale (Jones et al., 2011).

When communal narcissists were led to believe they would not have power, they indicated more intentions to cheat. When they were led to believe they would have power, they indicated less intentions to cheat. Thus, it seems that undermining a communal narcissists' sense of power alters intentions in their relationships. However, in the context of interpersonal relationships, future research needs to disentangle the differences between the perception of having relationship power and the perception of feeling powerful more generally.

7.3 Vulnerable Narcissism in Relationships

Research into the romantic lives of vulnerable narcissists is also sparse. What is known is that vulnerable narcissists experience higher attachment anxiety (Rohmann et al., 2012) and worry they will lose their partners to rivals (Hart et al., 2018). When asked why they purposely try to make their partners jealous, vulnerable narcissists offered several reasons (Tortoriello et al., 2017). First, they sought power and control over their partner. Second, after experiencing jealousy, they wanted revenge on the partner. This finding goes hand in hand with their own self-reports that they behave more negatively in response to relationship conflict (Drotleff & Brunell, 2020). Third, they used jealousy as a test of the relationship, to gain assurance of the partner's love or to make sure the relationship is strong. Lastly, they desired approval from the partner as a means of compensating for feelings of inadequacy. Thus, it seems that vulnerable narcissists try to make their partners feel vulnerable and insecure as a means of increasing their own feelings of self-worth. Furthermore, vulnerable narcissists appear to be less committed to their relationship partners as they report greater attention to relationship alternatives and lower relationship satisfaction (Drotleff & Brunell, 2020).

Although there is some evidence that narcissists can change if they are motivated to do so (Finkel et al., 2009; Hepper et al., 2014), there is no evidence so far that these changes last over longer periods of time. The information presented here, taken together, suggests that many relationships with narcissists, in general, are damaging. Not only is the relationship itself more likely to be destructive, but there are also potential negative consequences for the well-being of their partners who are left coping with damage they leave in their wake.

8 Are Narcissists Likeable?

Although there are plenty of reasons to avoid relationships with agentic and vulnerable narcissists, encountering narcissists in daily life is common. Given that ex-partners of agentic narcissists reported that at first they thought the agentic narcissist was attractive, charming, and fun (Brunell & Campbell, 2011), I next examine how likeable people perceive narcissists to be. I will then address narcissists' level of self-awareness about their off-putting qualities and how well they tolerate narcissistic qualities in others. Most of the research on these topics have examined agentic narcissism, but I include research on the other forms of narcissism when possible.

A stream of research has demonstrated a consistent pattern for agentic narcissists: They appear to be likeable upon first acquaintance, but their likeability deteriorates over time as they become more acquainted with their peers. Paulhus (1998) provided the seminal research on this topic. In two studies, he put unacquainted students into small groups for weekly class activities for seven weeks. He obtained peer ratings after the first and seventh weeks. At first agentic narcissists were rated as extraverted, confident, entertaining, and intelligent, but after the seventh meeting, they were deemed as less agreeable and warm (a proxy for likeability) and more prone to brag, overestimate their abilities, and behave more hostilely during the group activity.

Several researchers have investigated why agentic narcissists are able to make good first impressions. It seems that the most maladaptive aspects of agentic narcissism, entitlement and exploitativeness, elicit liking upon meeting

(Back et al., 2010). For example, more entitled and exploitative people were impeccably dressed, had friendly facial expressions, were self-assured in their body movement, and used humorous verbal expressions; all of these appear to be cues that draw others in. These cues are also likely to suggest an impression that one has more positive self-esteem (Giacomin & Jordan, 2019).

Thus, it seems that agentic narcissists' desire for admiration is paid off during the process of acquaintanceship. However, over time others expect them to become more intimate and cooperative, but they fail to meet this expectation (Back et al., 2010). Furthermore, they can become disruptive members of a group because of their impulsivity, difficulty delaying gratification, and focus on self-enhancement.

In other studies that put unacquainted individuals into groups and tracked them over time, it was found that higher agentic narcissists were more popular than lower agentic narcissists at the first encounter, equally popular as lower agentic narcissists upon second encounter, and less popular by the third encounter (Leckelt et al., 2015). Thus, while others become more popular among their peers as they get acquainted with others, this is not the case for agentic narcissists (Czarna et al., 2016). Not only do agentic narcissists' likeability sour over time, but they also rank high in unpopularity among well-acquainted people (although not especially low among popular group members) (Czarna et al., 2014). However, despite their status among the unpopular, they might not actively be disliked (Rentzsch & Gebauer, 2019).

Rentzsch and Gebauer (2019) investigated why agentic narcissists become less popular over time, arguing that their more insufferable personalities get in their way. However, they note that agentic narcissists are not the victims of their personalities, but rather play a more active role because they also like others less than low agentic narcissists do, a sentiment that is then reciprocated by others. In their study, student groups met for several hours per week to work on a project over the course of the term. Agentic narcissists liked others less and were liked by others less, supporting the study authors' hypothesis.

In a related vein, Küfner and colleagues (2013) propose a dual pathway model to better understand how and when agentic narcissists make good impressions on others. They suggest that one pathway concerns being seen by others as assertive and the other pathway entails being seen as aggressive. In one study, participants engaged in group conversations that were likely to elicit differences in opinion (e.g., decisions about a moral dilemma, how to arrange a shared living space). Afterward, they rated group members on their likeability, assertiveness, and aggressiveness. The results indicated that agentic narcissists were more popular when they were viewed as assertive and less popular when they were viewed as aggressive. When these dimensions get collapsed together, however, it would indicate that agentic narcissism and popularity are unrelated. In their follow-up study, these discussions were videotaped and coded for (a) expressiveness and dominance, (b) arrogance and combativeness, and (c) likeability. Narcissistic displays of dominance and expressiveness were seen as assertive and positively linked to popularity. Arrogant and combative behavior resulted in being seen as aggressive (because of more cynical remarks or disruptive behavior), which was linked to less popularity.

Thus, for the popularity of agentic narcissists, it appears that the situation matters. Küfner et al. (2013) contend that in superficial contexts, perhaps at first acquaintance, agentic narcissists tend to be seen as charming and likeable. However, in situations involving differences in opinion or decision making, agentic narcissists' darker qualities emerge.

Furthermore, there is a difference between popularity and social status, although they can coincide (Cheng et al., 2013). Both are also facilitated by extraversion at first acquaintance, which agentic narcissists have in abundance. However, status involves prominence, respect, and influence in the eyes of others (Anderson et al., 2006), which is likely to be maintained by agreeableness and empathy, two qualities that agentic narcissists lack. Popularity, on the other hand, concerns how much a person is liked by others; popularity tends to be maintained by communal traits such as interpersonal warmth and cooperation, which agentic narcissists also lack (Back et al., 2011). Thus, the distinction between social status and popularity can have consequences for agentic narcissists' social value and self-perceptions over time. In a set of studies, Carlson and DesJardin (2015) found that agentic narcissists initially gained social status but not necessarily popularity among their peers. Although agentic narcissists initially perceived themselves to gain both social status and popularity, they realized that they lost both over time, even though their social standing did not become especially low. One area of narcissistic misperception is that agentic narcissists seem to think that behaviors such as highlighting others' weaknesses, dominance, competitiveness, and arrogance bring them status, but in general people tend to value attributes such as trustworthiness, confidence, and likeability.

Extremely little research has examined the likeability of communal narcissists. The little that does exist suggests that communal narcissists are liked by others, but not more than those who are not communal narcissistic (Rentzsch & Gebauer, 2019). Communal narcissists also indicated more liking for their peers. Thus, it does not appear that communal narcissists have the same kind of interpersonal struggles that their agentic narcissistic and vulnerable narcissistic counterparts do.

What about liking for vulnerable narcissists? In a study by Hart and colleagues (2018), participants viewed a profile of a person who was vulnerable narcissistic and someone who was not. They were asked how likeable the traits associated with vulnerable narcissism were and how similar they thought they were to the targets. They were then asked questions about interpersonal attraction such as how willing they would be to introduce the target to others.

Overall, participants indicated that vulnerable narcissists were less similar to them and were rated as less likeable (Hart et al., 2018). However, participants who scored higher on vulnerable narcissism themselves indicated that the vulnerable narcissistic target was more similar to them and more likeable. Agentic narcissists indicated liking for the vulnerable narcissistic target, but only once self-esteem was taken into account. When Czarna et al. (2016) examined the social networks of vulnerable narcissists, they found that while vulnerable narcissists were less likely to be nominated for their likability, they also were not actively disliked by their peers. There was also a level of reciprocity as vulnerable narcissists also disliked their peers to a greater extent than less vulnerable narcissists did.

In sum, the research on likeability has demonstrated that narcissists are not particularly liked by their peers. In the case of agentic narcissists, specifically, through the process of acquaintanceship, others like them less over time because they lack warmth and are not cooperative while simultaneously revealing that they are arrogant, aggressive, and engage in high levels of self-enhancement, which are qualities that turn others off.

9 Do Trait Narcissists Have Self-Awareness?

Scholars have been conflicted about this question, but some research has helped shed some light, at least for agentic narcissists. In the past, some have argued that due to agentic narcissists' motivation to see themselves in an overly positive light, they are lacking in self-insight or misunderstand how they are perceived by others (Emmons, 1984; Morf & Rhodewalt, 2001). In a set of empirical studies, Carlson and colleagues (2011) sought to directly investigate this question. Specifically, they examined the extent to which agentic narcissists' meta-perceptions (i.e., the perceptions people have about how they are perceived by others) were as positive as their self-perceptions. Because considerable research has found that the likeability of agentic narcissists wanes over time (e.g., Paulhus, 1998), Carlson and colleagues (2011) examined the perceptions of people who were newly acquainted with the target person and compared them to those who knew the target person for a period of time. They also completed studies that examined newly acquainted groups over time. Results of their studies indicated that agentic narcissists were indeed aware that they have narcissistic qualities and that their self-perceptions were more positive than their meta-perceptions. Likewise, they were aware that their reputations sour among their peers over time. Their meta-perceptions were closer to their social realities, suggesting that agentic narcissists have some self-insight.

How, then, do agentic narcissists maintain their inflated self-views? Carlson and colleagues (Carlson et al., 2011; Carlson, 2013) argue that narcissists realize that they are more condescending, criticize others, argue, talk about themselves, and brag (among other qualities). Although they know these qualities are not socially desirable, agentic narcissists view them as *personally* desirable and ideal qualities to have because they believe these qualities bring about personal gain. Furthermore, another strategy agentic narcissists might adopt is to derogate others by thinking others are too dense to understand how great they are or blame it on jealousy.

Research has yet to investigate the extent to which communal and vulnerable narcissists have self-awareness. The research examining how well narcissists tolerate narcissistic qualities and behaviors in others has also focused exclusively on agentic narcissism.

10 Do Narcissists Tolerate Others?

In one study, agentic narcissists did a rating exercise on agentic narcissistic traits such as rude, selfish, aggressive, flashy, and arrogant (Hart & Adams, 2014). They also rated themselves on these traits. Consistent with previous research (Carlson et al., 2011), agentic narcissists were aware that they possessed agentic narcissistic traits. They also rated others who had these traits more favorably. It seems to be that agentic narcissists perceive other agentic narcissists as more likeable because they perceive other agentic narcissists as similar to themselves (Burton et al., 2017).

Perhaps there is a disconnect for agentic narcissists about what constitutes desirable behaviors. For example, agentic narcissists are prone to self-promotive behaviors. When they do so, are they trying to convince themselves of their own superiority or do they simply not care that their behavior alienates others (Morf & Rhodewalt, 2001; Paulhus & Williams, 2002; Wallace, 2011)? Another possibility is that they think they are making a good impression on others when they engage in self-promotion (Hart et al., 2016). Given that agentic narcissists find agentic traits to be desirable, they might believe that others do so as well. Therefore, they might believe it is desirable to demonstrate how they are competent and self-sufficient. Hart and colleagues (2016) completed a study in which participants were asked to rate how desirable agentic and communal traits were in making a good impression and their beliefs about the extent to which self-promotion facilitates making good impressions on others. They also reported on their own self-promotional tendencies. Their results suggested that agentic narcissists believed projecting agentic traits and engaging in self-promotion were effective in making a good impression. This finding could account for why they brag and exaggerate, stage performances, and otherwise show off.

Taken together, it might seem as though agentic narcissists are more accepting of narcissistic qualities in others. However, there is a bit of a paradox because agentic narcissists also appear to be sensitive to the slights from others and less forgiving of others' abrasiveness (Bushman & Baumeister, 1998; Exline et al., 2004; McCullough et al., 2003), the very aspects of which they seem to be accepting. There is even some evidence that agentic narcissists are exceptionally intolerant to others' antisocial acts even though they are willing to engage in the same behavior themselves (Wallace et al., 2016)! Adams and colleagues (Adams et al., 2015) proposed the concept of narcissistic hypocrisy, suggesting that agentic narcissists claim to be forgiving but have difficulty following through when they have to confront harsh or narcissistic behavior from others. For example, they seem to think they are tolerant of rude behavior of others when considered in more vague terms. However, when they are giving a clear, concrete example of behavior (honking and making aggressive gestures in traffic), agentic narcissists are less accepting of this behavior.

11 Frequently Asked Questions About Narcissism

As a professor and scholar, I am frequently engaged in presentations and conversations with others about narcissism, both inside and outside the academic setting. Narcissism has become such a "hot" topic that many people seek to better understand what it is and how it operates. In the following section, I detail the two most frequently asked questions I receive when engaging in discussions with others about narcissism.

11.1 Frequently Asked Question #1: Where Does Narcissism Come From?

11.1.1 Parenting and Agentic Narcissism

Most of the research examining the topic of the development of narcissism investigates how parents might socialize narcissism in their children (Thomaes et al., 2018), although narcissism is partly heritable (Luo & Cai, 2018).

One way that psychologists have examined parenting and the development of narcissism (more generally) is through the lens of four parenting styles: authoritarian/autocratic, authoritative/responsive, indulgent/permissive, and indifferent/uninvolved (Baumrind, 1971; 1980). A parent who is authoritarian/autocratic seeks to shape and control the child's behavior. They demand obedience and expect their orders to be obeyed without explanation and are highly punitive. These parents are demanding and lack adequate responsiveness. By contrast, authoritative/responsive parents are both demanding and responsive. What this means is that they provide clear standards for the child's conduct and use reasoning and explanation to influence the child's behavior. They consider their child's point of view and are assertive; the point of discipline is to be supportive, instead of punitive, in setting appropriate boundaries. The indulgent/permissive parent is responsive but not demanding. They struggle to set appropriate boundaries for their child. Because they find it easy to express affection and difficult to punish the child, their parenting style is too lenient. Lastly, indifferent/uninvolved parents are not demanding, but they are also not responsive and supportive of their child's needs. Indifferent/uninvolved parents expect the child to manage their problems on their own, encourage independence from the parent, and expect the child to take responsibility for themselves.

Kernberg (1998) argued that too much or too little demandingness without responsiveness to the child's needs creates a disruption to development. Both lead the child to feel incompetent because in these contexts the child is not allowed to develop their own skills, or they fail to develop the skills without the parents' guidance and assistance. When demandingness is appropriate and combined with responsiveness to the child's needs, the child develops skills, learns to self-regulate, and gains autonomy (George & Solomon, 1989).

Cramer (2011) discusses the importance of considering different periods of child development, noting that indulgence and demandingness in early childhood and in adolescence are qualitatively different and have different consequences because the physical and emotional needs are different during different developmental stages. For the very young child, parental indulgence might help the child gain a sense of trust in others and feel others are responsive to their needs. In adolescence, parental indulgence could foster entitlement. A lack of responsiveness and support interferes with healthy development because the child develops a model of self that they are inadequate and unworthy of support (George & Solomon, 1989; Kernberg, 1998). When demandingness of a young child is excessive, the parent is overly controlling, takes over the child's activities, and expects strict obedience (Baumrind, 1971). In this context, the child does not develop their own skills while also failing to learn to recognize their personal thoughts and feelings, resulting in their need to seek out approval from others. In adolescence, when the parent is overly demanding, they undermine the adolescent's personal sense of competence. The child might chronically seek out their parent's approval, and if the parent praises the child for meeting their high demands, the child might develop an inflated sense of self as "special" that can only be maintained through continual admiration by others.

Thus, to examine how parenting style is associated with the development of agentic narcissism, Cramer (2011) created a longitudinal study to investigate the extent to which preschool precursors of narcissism (i.e., the excessive need for attention and admiration, exhibitionism, impulsivity, aggression, and chronic violation of rules) and self-reported parenting styles predicted narcissism in these children during emerging adulthood. She found that early gratification of physical and psychological needs (either through authoritative or indulgent/permissive parenting) predicted the child growing into an adult who is ambitious, energetic, creative, and empathetic (Pincus & Lukowitsky, 2010; Russ et al., 2008; Wink, 1992). The authoritarian style negatively predicted this healthy development, while indifferent parenting was unrelated to healthy development, suggesting that it is the combination of the demanding, controlling nature of the parent, without sufficient gratification – rather than merely a lack of gratification – that interferes with healthy development (Cramer, 2011). Agentic narcissism was predicted by narcissistic precursors in early childhood but was qualified by the mother's (but not the father's) parenting style. When a young child has a predisposition toward narcissism, maternal responsiveness that is inadequate because it is too low in infancy or young childhood (i.e., authoritarian) or too high in adolescence (i.e., indulgence/permissive), and demandingness that is inadequate because it is too high in infancy and early childhood (i.e., authoritarian) or too little in adolescence (i.e., indulgence/permissive), predict the development of agentic narcissism.

In another longitudinal study, children and their parents were followed every six months for two years, starting when the children were between the ages of seven and eleven (Brummelman et al., 2015). Their study strongly supported the parental overvaluation view, which is when parents view their children as special and entitled to more than other children. When parents overvalued their children, these children became more agentic narcissistic over time (but not higher in self-esteem), demonstrating that parental overvaluation does not predict positive self-views, more generally, but rather agentic narcissism specifically. Even when controlling for the parents' levels of agentic narcissism, parental overvaluation robustly predicted increases in child agentic narcissism over time. Notably, children's perceptions of parental warmth were positively associated with children's self-esteem over time, but a lack of parental warmth did not predict child agentic narcissism over time. Others have likewise found that parental warmth was not related to agentic narcissism (Wetzel & Robins, 2016). Taken together, it seems that parental overvaluation predicts the development of agentic narcissism.

The research in this section discusses the role of parenting in the development of the agentic form of grandiose narcissism. No research to date has examined the role of parenting on the development of communal narcissism. In the following section, I highlight research that also includes the examination of vulnerable narcissism.

11.1.2 Parenting and Vulnerable Narcissism

Several retrospective studies examined the association between parenting practices and vulnerable narcissism, focusing on aspects such as parental invalidation, overparenting (or helicopter parenting), and psychological control (Green et al., 2020; Huxley & Bizumic, 2017; van Schie et al., 2020; Winner & Nicholson, 2018). Huxley and Bizumic (2017) examined parental invalidation, arguing that when parents fail to respect and validate the experiences and emotions of their children, the children fail to develop a means of experiencing these emotions. Instead, they focus on their parents' needs and working to gain admiration from others, eventually becoming excessively dependent on this admiration. They found that maternal and paternal invalidation was associated with both vulnerable and agentic narcissism when controlling for parental coldness, rejection, and overprotection as well as age and gender of the participant. A difference between agentic and vulnerable narcissism was for vulnerable narcissism, the other parenting variables were not significant predictors when invalidation was taken to account, but parental rejection and warmth were also significant predictors for agentic narcissism. Similar patterns were found in studies examining overparenting and psychological control (Green et al., 2020; van Schie et al., 2020; Winner & Nicholson, 2018). Although overparenting tends to be associated with warmth and responsiveness, these parents are also overinvolved and intrusive; their tendencies toward psychological control through guilt and manipulation diminish the child's ability to appropriately develop psychologically and emotionally. Van Schie et al. (2020) argued that overprotection limits the ability for children to learn from their own experience and makes them more reliant on feedback and guidance from others. When parents are too lenient, they likewise limit their children's ability to learn from experience because a lack of setting relevant boundaries inhibits the development of a sense of reality and self-discipline.

Because most research on parenting has relied on retrospective reports of parenting among adults, Mechanic and Barry (2015) asked adolescent participants to report on the parenting practices their parents use, including parental involvement (such as doing activities together), positive reinforcement (praise, rewards), inconsistent discipline, and monitoring (knowing where their children are and what they are doing). They also asked the participants' parents to report on their own parenting practices. In their study, vulnerable narcissism was related to adolescent reports of inconsistent discipline. Although agentic narcissism was correlated with their reports of parental involvement, positive reinforcement, and inconsistent discipline, only positive reinforcement was significant when controlling for the other factors. Parent reports indicated a relationship between adolescent agentic narcissism and parental involvement. The researchers argue that the overuse of some strategies may foster agentic narcissistic tendencies more than others. For example, overuse of positive reinforcement might foster a sense of superiority and grandiosity because the child learns they are worthy of rewards, praise, and attention.

The studies that have investigated the association between vulnerable narcissism and parenting have relied on the Pathological Narcissism Inventory (Pincus et al., 2009) to assess both grandiose and vulnerable narcissism. However, a criticism of this measure is that the grandiose narcissism facet captures a large amount of vulnerability, suggesting that the measure should be conceived of as a measure of narcissistic vulnerability or of vulnerable narcissism with a small dose of grandiose content rather than as a measure containing separate facets of grandiose and vulnerable narcissism (Miller et al., 2016). Doing so would make the patterns between parenting and the development of narcissism clearer.

Taken together, the research highlights the pathways for the development of narcissism. Although there is considerable nuance in the research, it appears that permissive parenting (especially in adolescence) and overvaluation of the child predicts the development of agentic narcissism. Parental invalidation, psychological control, and overprotection of the child are the factors that predict the development of vulnerable narcissism.

11.2 Frequently Asked Question #2: How Do I Navigate a Relationship with a Narcissist?

There is a plethora of discussions among practitioners, clinicians, and journalists about how to cope with narcissistic relationships. By contrast, the academic literature lacks investigation into feasible ways of coping with a narcissist. The recommendation to "just leave" a job or a marriage is often not a feasible solution. In the following sections, I review the literature that does exist (mostly focused on agentic narcissistic relationships) and some solutions by practitioners that are offered but need investigation.

11.2.1 The Workplace

Having an agentic narcissistic boss or supervisor creates a toxic workplace environment because the supervisor has more power but disregards the needs of subordinates (Morf & Rhodewalt, 2001), steals credit from them (Graham &

Cooper, 2013), and is prone to manipulation and exploitation (Brunell et al., 2013; Casale et al., 2019; Smith-Jentsch et al., 2019).

The subordinate tends to be deferential to the supervisor (Hochwarter & Thompson, 2012) because even small amounts of resistance can be met with a disproportionate amount of punishment, including job termination (Godkin & Allcorn, 2011). Thus, subordinates are likely to try to smooth things over when their agentic narcissistic supervisors become offended (DuBrin, 2012).

Ellen and colleagues (2019) argue that the ability to manage work-relevant resources can help buffer the negative effects of agentic narcissistic supervision. An agentic narcissistic supervisor might be inclined to limit their subordinates' access to resources, such as by hoarding resources for themselves, and consequently leaving their team without sufficient means to fulfill work demands. A person's ability to manage resources helps them protect the resources they have and acquire new resources, including access to equipment, assistance, flexibility, and control over their work (Frieder et al., 2015). Resource management ability increases effective coping because it gives subordinates a sense of personal control (Hochwarter et al., 2007). Ellen et al. (2019) argued that those with higher levels of resource management ability suffer less detriment because they are better able to conserve, acquire, and redirect stress-buffering assets to address demands that are inflicted by the agentic narcissistic supervisor, such as job tension, emotional exhaustion, depressed mood at work, and task performance. They have acquired a means to conserving their energy and getting assistance from their coworkers.

In order to ease the impact of a situation wherein subordinates have to engage their work-relevant resources to be productive and efficacious while working for an agentic narcissistic supervisor, Ellen et al. (2019) make several recommendations for organizations. The first concerns organizational policies, such as creating clear guidelines and policies about how resources are allocated (Cropanzano et al., 2007). Having clear procedures for career advancement and merit-based compensation policies that recognize and reward workers' contributions could be effective at minimizing an agentic narcissistic supervisor's abuse of power. Furthermore, with clear guidelines, agentic narcissists would be less likely to advance because they tend to be less effective in the workplace (Grijalva et al., 2015; Liu et al., 2022). The second concerns helping employees build their resources, such as by offering Employee Assistance Programs or other means to manage stressful situations. One focus in the workplace has been mindfulness training to help employees appraise situations more objectively and temper reactions that can become overwhelming and taxing (Hulsheger et al., 2013).

The research has indicated significant difficulty in trying to help the agentic narcissistic supervisor change the way they lead. For example, in a study of executive coaches working with agentic narcissistic leaders, coaches were recruited to report on why the leader needed coaching and the coaching strategies that were and were not effective in dealing with the agentic narcissistic client (Diller et al., 2021). Coaches described their agentic narcissistic clients as self-absorbed and easily offended. The coaches indicated that the leader needed coaching because they were having difficulties dealing with others or having communication issues, for professional reorientation, and for leadership improvement. From a list of coaching strategies that were provided by the researchers, coaches indicated that strategies of showing appreciation, building up trust, and mirroring the client's behavior were the most effective strategies when coaching the agentic narcissistic leader. An open-ended question also asked the coaches to explain the strategies that they thought were successful or unsuccessful when coaching the agentic narcissistic client. These strategies were then coded by the researchers. The results indicated that the successful and unsuccessful strategies varied highly and contradicted one another (i.e., a strategy that was suggested as successful by one coach was listed as unsuccessful by another), demonstrating that how to deal with an agentic narcissist remains unclear and seems to depend on trial and error. It is worth noting that the top successful strategies coaches mentioned were practicing mindfulness and using humor, indicating acceptance that they cannot change their client and focus instead on managing their own distress from the coaching relationship.

For these reasons, some argue that coaching an agentic narcissist is a wasted effort because they are too resistant to critical feedback (Bushman & Baumeister, 1998; Fehn & Schütz, 2021; Kernis & Sun, 1994). Because agentic narcissists frequently attribute problems to others rather than to themselves (O'Reilly & Hall, 2021; Stucke, 2003), they rarely see reasons to change (Brunell & Campbell, 2011). They could benefit from training in empathy, perspective taking, and emotional experience (Hepper et al., 2014), but they have to be open to these kinds of interventions to change their behavior. In the event that the agentic narcissist is able to see that hurting others harms their reputation, they might be willing to change because doing so would then boost their status and reinforce their grandiose self-views (Grapsas et al., 2019).

Because research has highlighted that agentic narcissists emerge as leaders (Brunell et al., 2008; Grijalva et al., 2015) but are not necessarily effective as leaders (Nevicka, Velden et al., 2011; Nevicka et al., 2018; Schmid et al., 2021), some argue that the changes should be made to how organizations select and promote job candidates rather than trying to change narcissistic behavior (Fehn & Schütz, 2021). One strategy could be to use valid personality tests and refrain from hiring agentic narcissists to leadership positions in the first place (Fehn & Schütz, 2021), although many organizations are reluctant to do so. A spin on this idea could be to select for personality traits such as integrity, empathy, and agreeableness, which do not align with narcissistic tendencies. Because agentic narcissists are likeable upon first encounter (Back et al., 2010; Giacomin & Jordan, 2019), they are likely to be successful in job interviews; conditional reasoning tests and objective performance measures could be incorporated into selection and promotion procedures to circumvent more subjective measures. Lastly, jobs that could be framed in terms of their communal aspects, which would deter agentic narcissists from applying simply because their self-views are more agentic.

A related topic to the agentic narcissistic boss is one of the agentic narcissistic mentor, who comes across to the protégé as a supporter but undermines them in passive-aggressive ways at the same time (Smith-Jentsch et al., 2019). For example, the agentic narcissistic mentor tends to give constructive criticism publicly rather than privately and praise tends to be delivered as a backhanded compliment. Frequently, the mentor only bothers to support the protégé when it is in the mentor's best interest and will not be bothered to mentor when it is not. These kinds of mentors are "trophy collectors" in the sense that every time their protégé is successful, it is akin to a trophy collected by the mentor to boast their own success. Professionally, such relationships are challenging because the mentor tends to have more power and the protégé may fear retribution should the protégé wish to terminate the relationship. To facilitate productive mentor–protégé relationships, Smith-Jentsch and colleagues (2019) offer the following advice to people looking for a mentor: (a) the protégé should learn as much as possible about a potential mentor beforehand, such as asking the person's previous proteges about their experiences. This could lessen the chances of finding oneself in a relationship with a narcissist. (b) The protégé can set realistic expectations for the relationship by discussing how much time and energy will be put into the mentoring relationship with the mentor. The protégé must keep in mind that an agentic narcissistic mentor will be helpful to the extent that their goals and those of the protégé align. The protégé must also keep in mind that agentic narcissistic mentors are not empathetic and can be harsh at times. They are best suited for someone who is able to take their feedback in stride. (c) Should the relationship come to an end, it is best to exit quickly and with as much grace as possible, which will limit retribution on the part of the mentor.

Furthermore, Smith-Jentsch and colleagues (2019) offer additional advice that can help buffer the relationship between the protégé and the mentor in any situation. For example, they suggest setting healthy boundaries around the topics that are discussed so that the lines between professional and personal relationships do not blur. Given that the mentor is giving their time and energy to the protégé, it's necessary for the protégé to express gratitude to them. Lastly, they recommend developing a network of mentors inside and outside of the organization that can provide different supports, such as expertise, information, and social support.

Although the research in this section focused on agentic narcissistic relationships in the workplace, the practical suggestions offered should help in any challenging relationship at work. However, research is needed focusing on communal and vulnerable narcissistic relationships in the workplace.

11.2.2 Interpersonal Relationships

Given how toxic relationships with narcissists can be, it makes sense to advise people to leave their relationships altogether (Durvasula, 2015). If narcissists – agentic narcissists in particular – think they are great the way they are and that others have the problem, why would they change? Even worse, typical suggestions for improving relationships might backfire when the relationship is with a narcissist – any kind of narcissist. For example, constructive responses to conflict tend to involve voice and loyalty (Rusbult & Zembrodt, 1983). Voice is when a person tries to improve the situation by actively and constructively discussing the situation or problem. Loyalty, by contrast, is when a person passively, but hopefully, waits for the situation or problem to blow over. These strategies tend to build intimacy (Overall & Sibley, 2008) as well as satisfaction and commitment (Rusbult et al., 1986). However, with a narcissistic partner, engaging in loyalty might simply strengthen their narcissistic tendencies. Using voice to address a problem might simply provoke the narcissist, who is motivated to defend themselves and blame others for problems (Malkin, 2015).

There is some promising research that has indicated that agentic narcissists can change for the better. One study demonstrated that when agentic narcissists were asked to make communal self-statements such as "I am a caring person" repeatedly, they temporarily became less entitled and exploitative (Jordan et al., 2014). Furthermore, when they spent time recalling a time when they "showed concern, love or acceptance for another person," the participants' agentic narcissism decreased over time (Jordan et al., 2014, p. 515). Another series of studies that were directed toward increasing empathy or priming interdependence reduced state narcissism and promoted an other focus (Giacomin & Jordan, 2014).

Other studies have examined the extent to which agentic narcissists could behave in more empathic or communal ways toward others. In one study, participants were randomly assigned to take someone else's perspective while others were not (Hepper et al., 2014). This study revealed that those who were asked to take someone else's perspective were more empathetic even when they were agentic narcissistic. This research highlights that agentic narcissists do not lack an ability to change their ways. Additional research examined agentic narcissists in ongoing relationships (Finkel et al., 2009). In one study, participants were primed with communal images such as a teacher helping a student. When narcissists were primed with these images, they subsequently reported greater commitment to their romantic partner (Finkel et al. 2009). In another study, married couples were asked how much their spouse elicits communal characteristics from them, such as being warm and nurturing, and were asked about their commitment four months later. When participants indicated that their spouse elicited communal qualities from them, they reported greater commitment to the marriage over time, an effect that was stronger for agentic narcissists. An additional study demonstrated that when the partners of agentic narcissists made them feel loved and cared for during a personal discussion, the agentic narcissist experienced greater relationship commitment following the interaction.

A recent study sought to combine communal activation activities with psychoeducational videos about healthy relationships to determine if agentic and vulnerable narcissists would report improved attitudes about relationship behaviors (Biesen & Smith, 2023). All participants saw psychoeducational videos about healthy relationships that included the topics of communication, trust, honesty, and mutual respect. Half of the participants were randomly assigned to think about a relationship issue they were having. They were first asked to think about their partner's perspective on the relationship issue and describe what the partner might be thinking or feeling. Second, they were asked to reflect on the similarities and differences they have from their partner and how these might serve as strengths and weaknesses in the relationship. Third, they were asked to think about a time when they behaved in a caring way toward their partner, even when stressed. Finally, they were asked how better ways of communicating could help resolve the relationship issue. They then responded to a series of questions about empathy for their partner, relationship commitment, desire for closeness, criticism toward the partner, communication patterns with their partner, and relationship satisfaction. The results indicated positive change in attitudes for vulnerable narcissists but not for grandiose narcissists, particularly with regard to negative communication patterns and commitment.

The lines of research described here show a lot of promise about the extent to which narcissists, in general, can change, but it remains unknown how long such effects last or how it works outside laboratory contexts. Yet some advice is to try to work with the concepts in real-life settings (Malkin, 2015). Malkin suggests using empathy prompts such as voicing how important the relationship is and revealing one's own vulnerable feelings (e.g., being sad, hurt, ashamed). When these prompts remind narcissists that they are important to their partners and are cared about, they might also elicit more communal feelings and behaviors from the narcissist. Malkin claims that the person will know their prompts have been successful if the narcissist responds in affirming and validating ways.

Before a person becomes too invested in a relationship, it might be wise to make the person aware of narcissistic qualities so they can identify if someone is narcissistic and decide if they want to get more involved. Once the person is involved in the relationship, it is too simplistic to advise them to leave. They may have plenty of reasons to stay, especially if they share resources such as finances and a home or have children together.

12 Conclusion and Further Directions

Narcissism is a complex personality trait marked by entitlement and antagonism. The most investigated form of narcissism is agentic grandiose narcissism. The evidence suggests that agentic narcissists are aware of their narcissistic qualities and view them as personally desirable despite the interpersonal costs they bring. Although agentic narcissists can make good first impressions, their reputations sour over time. There is plenty of research to suggest that ongoing relationships with agentic narcissists are stressful, even toxic.

Although a lot is known about the agentic form of grandiose narcissism, a lot less is known about communal grandiose narcissism and vulnerable narcissism. With respect to communal narcissism, given that measurement of the construct is fairly new, our understanding of it remains underdeveloped. For example, how does communal narcissism develop? What are the interpersonal consequences of interacting with a communal narcissist? Given that communal narcissists self-enhance in the communal domain, are relationships with communal narcissists positive, or are they akin to wolves in sheep's clothing by functioning more like their agentic counterparts? Future research is needed to better understand the interpersonal dynamics of communal narcissists.

By contrast, more is known about vulnerable narcissism than communal narcissism, but a lot less is known in comparison to agentic narcissism because vulnerable narcissism did not capture the attention of as many scholars early on as agentic narcissism did. Over the past decade more studies have investigated vulnerable narcissism, but more information is needed. Do they have the same kind of self-insights that agentic narcissists have? Are they aware of the stress they inflict on their relationship partners? Given that vulnerable narcissists tend to be shyer and more inhibited – qualities that might mask narcissism early on – how does one learn to "spot" a vulnerable narcissist?

Lastly, research examining how to cope in narcissistic relationships is sorely needed. What strategies are effective? Does it depend on the form of narcissism in question? Daily encounters with narcissists – all kinds of narcissists – are a common occurrence. Although narcissism is becoming increasingly understood, research is needed for "best practices" when interacting with a narcissist in daily life.

References

Ackerman, R. A., Witt, E. A., Donnellan, M. B. et al. (2011). What does the narcissistic personality inventory really measure? *Assessment, 18(1)*, 67–87. https://doi.org/10.1177/1073191110382845.

Adams, J. M., Hart, W., & Burton, K. A. (2015). I only like the idea of you: Narcissists tolerate others' narcissistic traits but not their corresponding behaviors. *Personality and Individual Differences*, *82*, 232–236. https://doi.org/10.1016/j.paid.2015.02.019.

Ainsworth, S. E., & Maner, J. K. (2012). Sex begets violence: Mating motives, social dominance, and physical aggression in men. *Journal of Personality and Social Psychology, 103(5)*, 819–829. https://doi-org.proxy.lib.ohio-state.edu/10.1037/a0029428.

Allen, T. D., Johnson, H., Rodopman, O. B., Ottinot, R. C., & Biga, A. (2009). Mentoring and protégé narcissistic entitlement. *Journal of Career Development, 35(4)*, 385–405. https://doi.org/10.1177/0894845308327735.

Altınok, A., & Kılıç, N. (2020). Exploring the associations between narcissism, intentions towards infidelity, and relationship satisfaction: Attachment styles as a moderator. *PLoS ONE, 15(11)*, 1–17, Article e0242277. https://doi.org.proxy.lib.ohio-state.edu/10.1371/journal.pone.0242277.

American Psychiatric Association. (1980). *Diagnostic and statistical manual of mental disorders* (3rd ed.). Washington, DC: American Psychiatric Association.

American Psychiatric Association. (2013). *Diagnostic and statistical manual of mental disorders* (5th ed.). Washington, DC: American Psychiatric Association. https://doi.org/10.1176/appi.books.9780890425596.

Anderson, C., Srivastava, S., Beer, J. S., & Spataro, S. (2006). Knowing your place: Self-perceptions of status in face-to-face groups. *Journal of Personality and Social Psychology, 91(6)*, 1094–1110. https://doi.org/10.1037/0022-3514.91.6.1094.

Arthur, C. A., Woodman, T., Ong, C. W., Hardy, L., & Ntoumanis, N. (2011). The role of athlete narcissism in moderating the relationship between coaches' transformational leader behaviors and athlete motivation. *Journal of Sport & Exercise Psychology, 33(1)*, 3–19. https://doi.org/10.1123/jsep.33.1.3.

Back, M. D., Baumert, A., Denissen, J. J. A. et al. (2011). PERSOC: A unified framework for understanding the dynamic interplay of personality and social relationships. *European Journal of Personality, 25(2)*, 90–107. https://doi.org/10.1002/per.811.

Back, M. D., Küfner, A. C. P., Dufner, M. et al. (2013). Narcissistic admiration and rivalry: Disentangling the bright and dark sides of narcissism. *Journal of Personality and Social Psychology, 105(6)*, 1013–1037. https://doi.org/10.1037/a0034431.

Back, M. D., Schmukle, S. C., & Egloff, B. (2010). Why are narcissists so charming at first sight? Decoding the narcissism – popularity link at zero acquaintance. *Journal of Personality and Social Psychology, 98(1)*, 132–145. https://doi.org/10.1037/a0016338.

Baumrind, D. (1971). Current patterns of parental authority. *Developmental Psychology, 4(1, Pt.2)*, 1–103. https://doi.org/10.1037/h0030372.

Baumrind, D. (1980). New directions in socialization research. *American Psychologist, 35(7)*, 639–652. https://doi.org/10.1037/0003-066X.35.7.639.

Benson, A., & Jordan, C. (2018). Narcissistic followership. In A. D. Hermann, A. B. Brunell, & J. D. Foster (Eds.), *The handbook of trait narcissism: Key advances, research methods, and controversies* (pp. 409–414). New York: Springer. https://doi.org/10.1007/978-3-319-92171-6.

Benson, A. J., Jordan, C. H., & Christie, A. M. (2016). Narcissistic reactions to subordinate role assignment: The case of the narcissistic follower. *Personality and Social Psychology Bulletin, 42(7)*, 985–999. https://doi.org/10.1177/0146167216649608.

Besser, A., & Priel, B. (2009). Emotional responses to a romantic partner's imaginary rejection: The roles of attachment anxiety, covert narcissism, and self-evaluation. *Journal of Personality, 77(1)*, 287–325. https://doi.org/10.1111/j.1467-6494.2008.00546.x.

Biesen, J. N., & Smith, D. A. (2023). Narcissism in romantic relationships: Using communal activation to promote relationship enhancing attitudes. *The Journal of Psychology, 157(8)*, 516–547. https://doi.org/10.1080/00223980.2023.2255925.

Bleske-Rechek, A., Remiker, M. W., & Baker, J. P. (2008). Narcissistic men and women think they are so hot – but they are not. *Personality and Individual Differences, 45(5)*, 420–424. https://doi.org/10.1016/j.paid.2008.05.018.

Blinkhorn, V., Lyons, M., & Almond, L. (2015). The ultimate femme fatale? Narcissism predicts serious and aggressive sexual coercive behaviour in females. *Personality and Individual Differences, 87*, 219–223. https://doi.org/10.1016/j.paid.2015.08.001.

Blinkhorn, V., Lyons, M., & Almond, L. (2016). Drop the bad attitude! Narcissism predicts acceptance of violent behaviour. *Personality and Individual Differences, 98*, 157–161. https://doi.org/10.1016/j.paid.2016.04.025.

Bogart, L. M., Benotsch, E. G., & Pavlovic, J. D. (2004). Feeling superior but threatened: The relation of narcissism to social comparison. *Basic and Applied Social Psychology, 26(1)*, 35–44. https://doi.org/10.1207/s15324834basp2601_4.

Bommer, W. H., Rich, G. A., & Rubin, R. S. (2005). Changing attitudes about change: Longitudinal effects of transformational leader behavior on employee cynicism about organizational change. *Journal of Organizational Behavior, 26(7)*, 733–753. https://doi.org/10.1002/job.342.

Boucher, K., Bégin, C., Gagnon-Girouard, M., & Ratté, C. (2015). The relationship between multidimensional narcissism, explicit and implicit self-esteem in eating disorders. *Psychology, 6(15)*, 2025–2039. https://doi.org/10.4236/psych.2015.615200.

Breeden, C. J., Hart, W., Kinrade, C., & Richardson, K. (2020). When you need identity management, people higher in some "dark" personalities can be your most thoughtful and altruistic helpers. *Personality and Individual Differences, 163(110052)*, 1–6. https://doi.org/10.1016/j.paid.2020.110052.

Brummelman, E., Thomaes, S., Nelemans, S. A. et al. (2015). Origins of narcissism in children. *Proceedings of the National Academy of Sciences of the United States of America, 112(12)*, 3659–3662. https://doi.org/10.1073/pnas.1420870112.

Brunell, A. B., & Buelow, M. T. (2019). Using the bogus pipeline to investigate trait narcissism and well-being. *Personality and Individual Differences, 151 (109509)*, 1–6. https://doi.org/10.1016/j.paid.2019.109509.

Brunell, A. B., & Campbell, W. K. (2011). Narcissism and romantic relationships: Understanding the paradox. In W. K. Campbell & J. D. Miller (Eds.), *Handbook of narcissism and narcissistic personality disorder: Theoretical approaches, empirical findings, and treatments* (pp. 344–350). Hoboken, NJ: John Wiley & Sons.

Brunell, A. B., Davis, M. S., Schley, D. R. et al. (2013). A new measure of interpersonal exploitativeness. *Frontiers in Psychology, 4(299)*, 1–9. https://doi.org/10.3389/fpsyg.2013.00299.

Brunell, A. B., Gentry, W. A., Campbell, W. K. et al. (2008). Leader emergence: The case of the narcissistic leader. *Personality and Social Psychology Bulletin, 34(12)*, 1663–1676. https://doi.org/10.1177/0146167208324101.

Buckels, E. E., Jones, D. N., & Paulhus, D. L. (2013). Behavioral confirmation of everyday sadism. *Psychological Science, 24(11)*, 2201–2209. https://doi.org/10.1177/0956797613490749.

Burton, K. A., Adams, J. M., Hart, W. et al. (2017). You remind me of someone awesome: Narcissistic tolerance is driven by perceived similarity. *Personality and Individual Differences*, *104*, 499–503. https://doi.org/10.1016/j.paid.2016.09.019.

Bushman, B. J., & Baumeister, R. F. (1998). Threatened egotism, narcissism, self-esteem, and direct and displaced aggression: Does self-love or self-hate lead to violence? *Journal of Personality and Social Psychology, 75(1)*, 219–229. https://doi.org/10.1037/0022-3514.75.1.219.

Campbell, W. K. (1999). Narcissism and romantic attraction. *Journal of Personality and Social Psychology, 77(6)*, 1254–1270. https://doi.org/10.1037/0022-3514.77.6.1254.

Campbell, W. K., Brunell, A. B., & Finkel, E. J. (2006). Narcissism, interpersonal self-regulation, and romantic relationships: An agency model approach. In K. D. Vohs & E. J. Finkel (Eds.), *Self and relationships: Connecting intrapersonal and interpersonal processes* (pp. 57–83). New York, NY: The Guilford Press.

Campbell, W. K., Bush, C. P., Brunell, A. B., & Shelton, J. (2005). Understanding the social costs of narcissism: The case of the tragedy of the commons. *Personality and Social Psychology Bulletin, 31(10)*, 1358–1368. https://doi.org/10.1177/0146167205274855.

Campbell, W. K., & Foster, C. A. (2002). Narcissism and commitment in romantic relationships: An investment model analysis. *Personality and Social Psychology Bulletin, 28(4)*, 484–495. https://doi.org/10.1177/0146167202287006.

Campbell, W. K., Foster, C. A., & Finkel, E. J. (2002). Does self-love lead to love for others? A story of narcissistic game playing. *Journal of Personality and Social Psychology, 83(2)*, 340–354. https://doi.org/10.1037/0022-3514.83.2.340.

Campbell, W. K., Hoffman, B. J., & Campbell, S. M. (2011). Narcissism in organizational contexts. *Human Resource Management Review, 21(4)*, 268–284. https://doi.org/10.1016/j.hrmr.2010.10.007.

Campbell, W. K., Reeder, G. D., Sedikides, C., & Elliot, A. J. (2000). Narcissism and comparative self-enhancement strategies. *Journal of Research in Personality, 34(3)*, 329–347. https://doi.org/10.1006/jrpe.2000.2282.

Campbell, W. K., Rudich, E. A., & Sedikides, C. (2002). Narcissism, self-esteem, and the positivity of self-views: Two portraits of self-love. *Personality and Social Psychology Bulletin, 28(3)*, 358–368. https://doi.org/10.1177/0146167202286007.

Carlson, E. N. (2013). Honestly arrogant or simply misunderstood? Narcissists' awareness of their narcissism. *Self and Identity, 12(3)*, 259–277. https://doi.org/10.1080/15298868.2012.659427.

Carlson, E. N., & DesJardin, N. M. L. (2015). Do mean guys always finish first or just say they do? Narcissists' awareness of their social status and popularity over time. *Personality and Social Psychology Bulletin, 41(7)*, 901–917. https://doi.org/10.1177/0146167215581712.

Carlson, K. S., & Gjerde, P. F. (2009). Preschool personality antecedents of narcissism in adolescence and young adulthood: A 20-year longitudinal study. *Journal of Research in Personality, 43(4)*, 570–578. https://doi.org/10.1016/j.jrp.2009.03.003.

Carlson, E. N., Vazire, S., & Oltmanns, T. F. (2011). You probably think this paper's about you: Narcissists' perceptions of their personality and reputation. *Journal of Personality and Social Psychology, 101(1)*, 185–201. https://doi.org/10.1037/a0023781.

Casale, S., Rugai, L., Giangrasso, B., & Fioravanti, G. (2019). Trait-emotional intelligence and the tendency to emotionally manipulate others among grandiose and vulnerable narcissists. *The Journal of Psychology: Interdisciplinary and Applied, 153(4)*, 402–413. https://doi.org/10.1080/00223980.2018.1564229.

Chan, C. Y., & Cheung, K. L. (2022). Exploring the gender difference in relationships between narcissism, competitiveness, and mental health problems among college students. *Journal of American College Health, 40(4)*, 1169–1178. https://doi.org/10.1080/07448481.2020.1788565.

Chatterjee, A., & Hambrick, D. (2007). It's all about me: Narcissistic CEOs and their effects on company strategy and performance. *Administrative Science Quarterly, 52(3)*, 351–386. https://doi.org/10.2189/asqu.52.3.351.

Chen, Y., Ferris, D. L., Kwan, H. K. et al. (2013). Self-love's lost labor: A self-enhancement model of workplace incivility. *Academy of Management Journal, 56(4)*, 1199–1219. https://doi.org/10.5465/amj.2010.0906.

Cheng, J. T., Tracy, J. L., Foulsham, T., Kingstone, A., & Henrich, J. (2013). Two ways to the top: Evidence that dominance and prestige are distinct yet viable avenues to social rank and influence. *Journal of Personality and Social Psychology, 104(1)*, 103–125. https://doi.org/10.1037/a0030398.

Chin, K., Atkinson, B. E., Raheb, H., Harris, E., & Vernon, P. A. (2017). The dark side of romantic jealousy. *Personality and Individual Differences, 115*, 23–29. https://doi.org/10.1016/j.paid.2016.10.003.

Chopik, W. J., & Grimm, K. J. (2019). Longitudinal changes and historic differences in narcissism from adolescence to older adulthood. *Psychology and Aging, 34(8)*, 1109–1123. https://doi.org/10.1037/pag0000379.

Chukwuorji, J. C., Uzuegbu, C. N., Agbo, F., Ifeagwazi, C. M. & Ebulum, G. C. (2020). Different slopes for different folks: Gender moderates the relationship between empathy and narcissism. *Current Psychology, 39*, 1808–1818. https://doi.org/10.1007/s12144-018-9881-z.

Conger, J. A. (1997). The dark side of leadership. In R. P. Vecchio (Ed.), *Leadership: Understanding the dynamics of power and influence in organizations* (pp. 199–215). Notre Dame, IN: University of Notre Dame Press.

Cramer, P. (2011). Young adult narcissism: A 20 year longitudinal study of the contribution of parenting styles, preschool precursors of narcissism, and denial. *Journal of Research in Personality, 45(1)*, 19–28. https://doi.org/10.1016/j.jrp.2010.11.004.

Cropanzano, R., Bowen, D. E., & Gilliland, S. W. (2007). The management of organizational justice. *The Academy of Management Perspectives*, *21(4)*, 34–48. https://doi.org/10.5465/AMP.2007.27895338.

Crowe, M. L., Lynam, D. R., Campbell, W. K., & Miller, J. D. (2019). Exploring the structure of narcissism: Toward an integrated solution. *Journal of Personality, 87(6)*, 1151–1169. https://doi.org/10.1111/jopy.12464.

Czarna, A. Z., Dufner, M., & Clifton, A. D. (2014). The effects of vulnerable and grandiose narcissism on liking-based and disliking-based centrality in social networks. *Journal of Research in Personality, 50*, 42–45. https://doi.org/10.1016/j.jrp.2014.02.004.

Czarna, A. Z., Leifeld, P., Śmieja, M., Dufner, M., & Salovey, P. (2016). Do narcissism and emotional intelligence win us friends? Modeling dynamics of peer popularity using inferential network analysis. *Personality and Social Psychology Bulletin, 42(11)*, 1588–1599. https://doi.org/10.1177/0146167216666265.

Davis, M. H. (1980). A multidimensional approach to individual differences in empathy. *JSAS Catalog of Selected Documents in Psychology, 10*, 85–104.

Dean, J. W., Brandes, P., & Dharwadkar, R. (1998). Organizational cynicism. *The Academy of Management Review, 23(2)*, 341–352. https://doi.org/10.2307/259378.

Diller, S. J., Frey, D., & Jonas, E. (2021). Coach me if you can! Dark triad clients, their effect on coaches, and how coaches deal with them. *Coaching: An International Journal of Theory, Research, and Practice, 14(2)*, 110–126. https://doi.org/10.1080/17521882.2020.1784973.

Donnellan, M. B., Trzesniewski, K. H., & Robins, R. W. (2009). An emerging epidemic of narcissism or much ado about nothing? *Journal of Research in Personality, 43(3)*, 498–501. https://doi.org/10.1016/j.jrp.2008.12.010.

Drotleff, C., & Brunell, A. B. (2020, February). *Patterns of relationship behaviors among grandiose and communal narcissists*. Poster presented at the annual meeting of the Society of Personality and Social Psychology, New Orleans, LA.

DuBrin, A. J. (2012). *Narcissism in the workplace: Research, opinion, and practice*. Northampton, MA: Edward Elgar.

Durvasula, R. (2015). *Should I stay or should I go? Surviving a relationship with a narcissist*. New York, NY: Post Hill Press.

Edwards, B. G., Albertson, E., & Verona, E. (2017). Dark and vulnerable personality trait correlates of dimensions of criminal behavior among adult offenders. *Journal of Abnormal Psychology, 126(7)*, 921–927. https://doi.org/10.1037/abn0000281.

Ellen, B. P., Kiewitz, C., Garcia, P. R. J. M., & Hochwarter, W. A. (2019). Dealing with the full-of-self boss: Interactive effects of supervisor narcissism and subordinate resource management ability on work outcomes. *Journal of Business Ethics, 157(3)*, 847–864. https://psycnet.apa.org/doi/10.1007/s10551-017-3666-4.

Emmons, R. A. (1984). Factor analysis and construct validity of the narcissistic personality inventory. *Journal of Personality Assessment, 48(3)*, 291–300. https://doi.org/10.1207/s15327752jpa4803_11.

Erkutlu, H., & Chafra, J. (2017). Leaders' narcissism and organizational cynicism in healthcare organizations. *International Journal of Workplace Health Management, 10(5)*, 346–363. https://doi.org/10.1108/IJWHM-12-2016-0090.

Exline, J. J., Baumeister, R. F., Bushman, B. J., Campbell, W. K., & Finkel, E. J. (2004). Too proud to let go: Narcissistic entitlement as a barrier to forgiveness. *Journal of Personality and Social Psychology, 87(6)*, 894–912. https://doi.org/10.1037/0022-3514.87.6.894.

Fatfouta, R. (2021). What do they really want? Effects of the wording of job advertisements on narcissists' perceptions of organizational attraction. *Current Psychology, a Journal for Diverse Perspectives on Diverse Psychological Issues*, *42*, 154–164. https://doi.org/10.1007/s12144-020-01332-9.

Fehn, T., & Schütz, A. (2021). What you get is what you see: Other-rated but not self-rated leaders' narcissistic rivalry affects followers negatively. *Journal of Business Ethics, 174(3)*, 549–566. https://doi.org/10.1007/s10551-020-04604-3.

Finkel, E. J., Campbell, W. K., Buffardi, L. E., Kumashiro, M., & Rusbult, C. E. (2009). The metamorphosis of Narcissus: Communal activation promotes relationship commitment among narcissists. *Personality and Social Psychology Bulletin, 35(10)*, 1271–1284. https://doi.org/10.1177/0146167209340904.

Foster, J. D., & Brunell, A. B. (2018). Narcissism and romantic relationships. In A. D. Hermann, A. B. Brunell, & J. D. Foster (Eds.), *The handbook of trait narcissism: Key advances, research methods, and controversies* (pp. 317–326). New York: Springer. https://doi.org/10.1007/978-3-319-92171-6.

Foster, J. D., Campbell, W. K., & Twenge, J. M. (2003). Individual differences in narcissism: Inflated self-views across the lifespan and around the world.

Journal of Research in Personality, 37(6), 469–486. https://doi.org/10.1016/S0092-6566(03)00026-6.

Foster, J. D., Shrira, I., & Campbell, W. K. (2006). Theoretical models of narcissism, sexuality, and relationship commitment. *Journal of Social and Personal Relationships, 23(3)*, 367–386. https://doi.org/10.1177/0265407506064204.

Freud, S. (1914/1991). On narcissism: An introduction. In J. Sandler, E. S. Person, & P. Fonagy (Eds.), *Freud's "On narcissism: An introduction"* (pp. 3–32). New Haven, CT: Yale University Press.

Frieder, R. E., Hochwarter, W. A., & DeOrtentiis, P. S. (2015). Attenuating the negative effects of abusive supervision: The role of proactive voice behavior and resource management ability. *The Leadership Quarterly, 26(5)*, 821–837. https://doi.org/10.1016/j.leaqua.2015.06.001.

Furnham, A., Richards, S. C., & Paulhus, D. L. (2013). The Dark Triad of personality: A 10 year review. *Social and Personality Psychology Compass, 7(3)*, 199–216. https://doi.org/10.1111/spc3.12018.

Gabriel, M. T., Critelli, J. W., & Ee, J. S. (1994). Narcissistic illusions in self-evaluations of intelligence and attractiveness. *Journal of Personality, 62(1)*, 143–155. https://doi.org/10.1111/j.1467-6494.1994.tb00798.x.

Galvin, B. M., Waldman, D. A., & Balthazard, P. (2010). Visionary communication qualities as mediators of the relationship between narcissism and attributions of leader charisma. *Personnel Psychology, 63(3)*, 509–537. https://doi.org/10.1111/j.1744-6570.2010.01179.x.

Gebauer, J. E., & Sedikides, C. (2018). Agency and communion in grandiose narcissism. In A. E. Abele & B. Wojciszke (Eds.), *Agency and Communion in Social Psychology* (pp. 90–102). New York: Routledge.

Gebauer, J. E., Sedikides, C., Verplanken, B., & Maio, G. R. (2012). Communal narcissism. *Journal of Personality and Social Psychology, 103(5)*, 854–878. https://doi.org/10.1037/a0029629.

Georgc, C., & Solomon, J. (1989). Internal working models of caregiving and security of attachment at age six. *Infant Mental Health Journal, 10(3)*, 222–237. https://doi.org/10.1002/1097-0355(198923)10:3<222::AID-IMHJ2280100308>3.0.CO;2-6.

Gerstner, W.-C., König, A., Enders, A., & Hambrick, D. C. (2013). CEO narcissism, audience engagement, and organizational adoption of technological discontinuities. *Administrative Science Quarterly, 58(2)*, 257–291. https://doi.org/10.1177/0001839213488773.

Gewirtz-Meydan, A. (2017). Why do narcissistic individuals engage in sex? Exploring sexual motives as a mediator for sexual satisfaction and function. *Personality and Individual Differences, 105*, 7–13. https://doi.org/10.1016/j.paid.2016.09.009.

Giacomin, M., & Jordan, C. H. (2014). Down-regulating narcissistic tendencies: Communal focus reduces state narcissism. *Personality and Social Psychology Bulletin, 40(4)*, 488–500. https://doi.org/10.1177/0146167213516635.

Giacomin, M., & Jordan, C. H. (2015). Validating power makes communal narcissists less communal. *Self and Identity, 14(5)*, 583–601. https://doi.org/10.1080/15298868.2015.1031820.

Giacomin, M., & Jordan, C. H. (2019). Misperceiving grandiose narcissism as self-esteem: Why narcissists are well-liked at zero acquaintance. *Journal of Personality, 87(4)*, 824–842. https://doi.org/10.1111/jopy.12436.

Glad, B. (2002). Why tyrants go too far: Malignant narcissism and absolute power. *Political Psychology, 23(1)*, 1–37. www.jstor.org/stable/3792241.

Godkin, L., & Allcorn, S. (2011). Organizational resistance to destructive narcissistic behavior. *Journal of Business Ethics, 104(4)*, 559–570. www.jstor.org/stable/41476327.

Gordon, K. H., & Dombeck, J. J. (2010). The associations between two facets of narcissism and eating disorder symptoms. *Eating behaviors, 11(4)*, 288–292. https://doi.org/10.1016/j.eatbeh.2010.08.004.

Graham, W. J., & Cooper, W. H. (2013). *Taking credit. Journal of Business Ethics, 115(2)*, 403–425. www.jstor.org/stable/42001991.

Grapsas, S., Brummelman, E., Back, M. D., & Denissen, J. J. A. (2019). The "why" and "how" of narcissism: A process model of narcissistic status pursuit. *Perspectives on Psychological Science, 15(1)*, 150–172. https://doi.org/10.1177/1745691619873350.

Green, A., MacLean, R., & Charles, K. (2020). Recollections of parenting styles in the development of narcissism: The role of gender. *Personality and Individual Differences, 167(110246)*, 1–6. https://doi.org/10.1016/j.paid.2020.110246.

Grijalva, E., Harms, P. D., Newman, D. A., Gaddis, B. H., & Fraley, R. C. (2015). Narcissism and leadership: A meta-analytic review of linear and nonlinear relationships. *Personnel Psychology, 68(1)*, 1–47. https://doi.org/10.1111/peps.12072.

Grijalva, E., & Newman, D. A. (2015). Narcissism and counterproductive work behavior (CWB): Meta-analysis and consideration of collectivist culture, big five personality, and narcissism's facet structure. *Applied Psychology: An International Review, 64(1)*, 93–126. https://doi.org/10.1111/apps.12025.

Grijalva, E., & Zhang, L. (2016). Narcissism and self-insight: A review and meta-analysis of narcissists' self-enhancement tendencies. *Personality and Social Psychology Bulletin, 42(1)*, 3–24. https://doi.org/10.1177/0146167215611636.

Grosz, M. P., Dufner, M., Back, M. D., & Denissen, J. J. A. (2015). Who is open to a narcissistic romantic partner? The roles of sensation seeking, trait anxiety, and similarity. *Journal of Research in Personality*, *58*, 84–95. https://doi.org/10.1016/j.jrp.2015.05.007.

Grosz, M. P., Göllner, R., Rose, N. et al. (2019). The development of narcissistic admiration and Machiavellianism in early adulthood. *Journal of Personality and Social Psychology*, *116(3)*, 467–482. https://doi.org/10.1037/pspp0000174.

Ha, S.-B., Lee, S., Byun, G., & Dai, Y. (2020). Leader narcissism and subordinate change-oriented organizational citizenship behavior: Overall justice as a moderator. *Social Behavior and Personality: An International Journal*, *48(7)* 1–13, e9330. https://doi.org/10.2224/sbp.9330.

Hansen-Brown, A. A. (2018). Perceived control theory of narcissism. In A. D. Hermann, A. B. Brunell, & J. D. Foster (Eds.), *The handbook of trait narcissism: Key advances, research methods, and controversies* (pp. 27–35). New York: Springer. https://doi.org/10.1007/978-3-319-92171-6.

Hart, W., & Adams, J. M. (2014). Are narcissists more accepting of others' narcissistic traits? *Personality and Individual Differences*, *64*, 163–167. https://doi.org/10.1016/j.paid.2014.02.038.

Hart, W., Adams, J. M., & Burton, K. A. (2016). Narcissistic for the people: Narcissists and Non-narcissists disagree about how to make a good impression. *Personality and Individual Differences*, *91*, 69–73. https://doi.org/10.1016/j.paid.2015.11.045.

Hart, W., Richardson, K., & Tortoriello, G. K. (2018). Grandiose and vulnerable narcissists disagree about whether others' vulnerable narcissism is relatable and tolerable. *Personality and Individual Differences*, *134*, 143–148. https://doi.org/10.1016/j.paid.2018.06.016.

Haslam, M., Mountford, V., Meyer, C., & Waller, G. (2008). Invalidating childhood environments in anorexia and bulimia nervosa. *Eating Behaviors*, *9(3)*, 313–318. https://doi.org/10.1016/j.eatbeh.2007.10.005.

Hawk, S. T., van den Eijnden, R. J. J. M, van Lissa, C. J., & ter Bogt, T. F. M. (2019). Narcissistic adolescents' attention-seeking following social rejection: Links with social media disclosure, problematic social media, and smartphone stress. *Computers in Human Behavior*, *92*, 65–75. https://doi.org/10.1016/j.chb.2018.10.032.

Hendin, H. M., & Cheek, J. M. (1997). Assessing hypersensitive narcissism: A reexamination of Murray's Narcism Scale. *Journal of Research in Personality*, *31(4)*, 588–599. https://doi.org/10.1006/jrpe.1997.2204.

Hepper, E. G., Hart, C. M., & Sedikides, C. (2014). Moving Narcissus: Can narcissists be empathic? *Personality and Social Psychology Bulletin*, *40(9)*, 1079–1091. https://doi.org/10.1177/0146167214535812.

Hill, P. L., & Roberts, B. W. (2012). Narcissism, well-being, and observer-rated personality across the lifespan. *Social Psychological and Personality Science, 3(2)*, 216–223. https://doi.org/10.1177/1948550611415867.

Hochwarter, W. A., Perrewé, P. L., Meurs, J. A., & Kacmar, C. (2007). The interactive effects of work-induced guilt and ability to manage resources on job and life satisfaction. *Journal of Occupational Health Psychology, 12*(2), 125–135. https://doi-org.proxy.lib.ohio-state.edu/10.1037/1076-8998.12.2.125.

Hochwarter, W. A., & Thompson, K. W. (2012). Mirror, mirror on my boss's wall: Engaged enactment's moderating role on the relationship between perceived narcissistic supervision and work outcomes. *Human Relations, 65(3)*, 335–366. https://doi.org/10.1177/0018726711430003.

House, R. J., Hanges, P. J., Jayidan, M. et al. (2004). *Leadership, culture, and organizations: The GLOBE study of 62 nations*. Thousand Oaks, CA: Sage.

Hulsheger, U. R., Alberts, H. J., Feinholdt, A., & Lang, J. W. (2013). Benefits of mindfulness at work: The role of mindfulness in emotion regulation, emotional exhaustion, and job satisfaction. *Journal of Applied Psychology, 98(2)*, 310–325. https://doi.org/10.1037/a0031313.

Huxley, E., & Bizumic, B. (2017). Parental invalidation and the development of narcissism. *The Journal of Psychology, 151(2)*, 130–147. https://doi.org/10.1080/00223980.2016.1248807.

Jauk, E., Neubauer, A. C., Mairunteregger, T. et al. (2016). How alluring are dark personalities? The Dark Triad and attractiveness in speed dating. *European Journal of Personality, 30(2)*, 125–138. https://doi.org/10.1002/per.2040.

Johnson, L. K., Plouffe, R. A., & Saklofske, D. H. (2019). Subclinical sadism and the Dark Triad: Should there be a Dark Tetrad? *Journal of Individual Differences, 40(3)*, 127–133. https://doi.org/10.1027/1614-0001/a000284.

Jones, D. N., Olderbak, S. G., & Figueredo, A. J. (2011). The intentions towards infidelity scale. In T. D. Fisher, C. M. Davis, W. L. Yarber, & S. L. Davis (Eds.), *Handbook of sexuality-related measures (3rd ed.)* (pp. 251–253). New York, NY: Routledge.

Jones, D. N., & Paulhus, D. L. (2010). Different provocations trigger aggression in narcissists and psychopaths. *Social Psychological and Personality Science, 1(1)*, 12–18. https://doi.org/10.1177/1948550609347591.

Jordan, C. H., Giacomin, M., & Kopp, L. (2014). Let go of your (inflated) ego: Caring more about others reduces narcissistic tendencies. *Social and Personality Psychology Compass, 8(9)*, 511–523. https://doi.org/10.1111/spc3.12128.

Judge, T. A., LePine, J. A., & Rich, B. L. (2006). Loving yourself abundantly: Relationship of the narcissistic personality to self- and other perceptions of workplace deviance, leadership, and task and contextual performance. *Journal of Applied Psychology, 91(4)*, 762–776. https://doi.org/10.1037/0021-9010.91.4.762.

Judge, T. A., Piccolo, R. F., & Kosalka, T. (2009). The bright and dark sides of leader traits: A review and theoretical extension of the leader trait paradigm. *The Leadership Quarterly, 20(6)*, 855–875. https://doi.org/10.1016/j.leaqua.2009.09.004.

Kajonius, P. J., & Bjorkman, T. (2020). Dark malevolent traits and everyday perceived stress. *Current Psychology: A Journal for Diverse Perspectives on Diverse Psychological Issues*, *39*, 2351–2356. https://doi.org/10.1007/s12144-018-9948-x.

Kardum, I., Hudek-Knezevic, J., Schmitt, D. P., & Grundler, P. (2015). Personality and mate poaching experiences. *Personality and Individual Differences*, *75*, 7–12. https://doi.org/10.1016/j.paid.2014.10.048.

Kausel, E. E., Culbertson, S. S., Leiva, P. I., Slaughter, J. E., & Jackson, A. T. (2015). Too arrogant for their own good? Why and when narcissists dismiss advice. *Organizational Behavior and Human Decision Processes*, *131*, 33–50. https://doi.org/10.1016/j.obhdp.2015.07.006.

Kernberg, O. F. (1970). Factors in the psychoanalytic treatment of narcissistic personalities. *Journal of the American Psychoanalytic Association, 18(1)*, 51–85. https://doi.org/10.1177/000306517001800103

Kernberg, P. F. (1998). Developmental aspects of normal and pathological narcissism. In E. F. Ronningstam (Ed.), *Disorders of narcissism: Diagnostic, clinical and empirical implications* (pp. 103–120). Washington, DC: American Psychiatric Association.

Kernberg, O. F. (1975). *Borderline conditions and pathological narcissism*. New York: Jason Aronson.

Kernis, M. H., & Sun, C.-R. (1994). Narcissism and reactions to interpersonal feedback. *Journal of Research in Personality, 28(1)*, 4–13. https://doi.org/10.1006/jrpe.1994.1002.

Kohut, H. (1971). *The analysis of self*. New York: International Universities Press.

Krizan, Z., & Herlache, A. D. (2018). The narcissism spectrum model: A synthetic view of narcissistic personality. *Personality and Social Psychology Review, 22(1)*, 3–31. https://doi.org/10.1177/1088868316685018.

Küfner, A. C. P., Nestler, S., & Back, M. D. (2013). The two pathways to being an (un-)popular narcissist. *Journal of Personality, 81(2)*, 184–195. https://doi.org/10.1111/j.1467-6494.2012.00795.x.

Lahey, B. B. (2009). Public health significance of neuroticism. *American Psychologist, 64(4)*, 241–256. https://doi.org/10.1037/a0015309.

Lamkin, J., Lavner, J. A., & Shaffer, A. (2017). Narcissism and observed communication in couples. *Personality and Individual Differences*, *105*, 224–228. https://doi.org/10.1016/j.paid.2016.09.046.

Lammers, J., Stoker, J. I., Jordan, J., Pollmann, M., & Stapel, D. A. (2011). Power increases infidelity among men and women. *Psychological Science*, *22(9)*, 1191–1197. https://doi-org.proxy.lib.ohio-state.edu/10.1177/0956797611416252.

Lata, M., & Chaudhary, R. (2020). Dark Triad and instigated incivility: The moderating role of workplace spirituality. *Personality and Individual Differences*, *166(110090)*, 1–6. https://doi.org/10.1016/j.paid.2020.110090.

Lavner, J. A., Lamkin, J., Miller, J. D., Campbell, W. K., & Karney, B. R. (2016). Narcissism and newlywed marriage: Partner characteristics and marital trajectories. *Personality Disorders: Theory, Research, and Treatment*, *7(2)*, 169–179. https://doi.org/10.1037/per0000137.

Leckelt, M., Küfner, A. C. P., Nestler, S., & Back, M. D. (2015). Behavioral processes underlying the decline of narcissists' popularity over time. *Journal of Personality and Social Psychology*, *109(5)*, 856–871. https://doi.org/10.1037/pspp0000057.

Lee, S. A. (2019). The Dark Tetrad and callous reactions to mourner grief: Patterns of annoyance, boredom, entitlement, schadenfreude, and humor. *Personality and Individual Differences*, *137*, 97–100. https://doi.org/10.1016/j.paid.2018.08.019.

Lee, K., & Ashton, M. C. (2005). Psychopathy, Machiavellianism, and Narcissism in the Five-Factor model and the HEXACO model of personality structure. *Personality and Individual Differences*, *38(7)*, 1571–1582. https://doi.org/10.1016/j.paid.2004.09.016.

Lee, K., & Ashton, M. C. (2012). *The H factor of personality: Why some people are manipulative, self-entitled, materialistic, and exploitative – and why it matters for everyone*. Waterloo: Wilfrid Laurier Press.

Lee, K., Ashton, M. C., Wiltshire, J. et al. (2013). Sex, power, and money: Prediction from the dark triad and honesty-humility. *European Journal of Personality*, *27(2)*, 145–154. https://doi.org/10.1002/per.1860.

Lee, R. M., Dean, B. L., & Jung, K. (2008). Social connectedness, extraversion, and subjective well-being: Testing a mediational model. *Personality and Individual Differences*, *45(5)*, 414–419. https://doi.org/10.1016/j.paid.2008.05.017.

Liu, X., Zheng, X., Li, N. et al. (2022). Both a curse and a blessing? A social cognitive approach to the paradoxical effects of leader narcissism. *Human Relations*, *75(11)*, 2011–2038. https://doi.org/10.1177/00187267211015925.

Luo, Y. L. L., & Cai, H. (2018). The Etiology of narcissism: A review of behavioral genetic studies. In A. T. Hermann, A. B. Brunell, & J. D. Foster (Eds.), *The handbook of trait narcissism: Key advances, research methods, and controversies* (pp. 97–104). New York, NY: Springer. https://doi.org/10.1007/978-3-319-92171-6.

Lynam, D. R., & Derefinko, K. J. (2006). Psychopathy and personality. In C. J. Patrick (Ed.), *Handbook of psychopathy* (pp. 133–155). New York, NY: The Guilford Press.

Maccoby, M. (2000). Narcissistic leaders: The incredible pros, the inevitable cons. *The Harvard Business Review, 78*, 68–78. https://hbr.org/2004/01/narcissistic-leaders-the-incredible-pros-the-inevitable-cons.

Mahler, M. S. (1963). Thoughts about development and individuation. *The Psychoanalytic Study of the Child, 18*, 307–324. https://doi.org/10.1080/00797308.1963.11822933.

Malkin, C. (2015). *Rethinking narcissism: The secret to recognizing and coping with narcissists*. New York, NY: Harper.

March, E., Litten, V., Sullivan, D. H., & Ward, L. (2020). Somebody that I (used to) know: Gender and dimensions of dark personality traits as predictors of intimate partner cyberstalking. *Personality and Individual Differences, 163 (110084),* 1–6. https://doi.org/10.1016/j.paid.2020.110084.

Marcus, D. K., Zeigler-Hill, V., Mercer, S. H., & Norris, A. L. (2014). The psychology of spite and the measurement of spitefulness. *Psychological Assessment, 26(2)*, 563–574. https://doi.org/10.1037/a0036039.

McCullough, M. E., Emmons, R. A., Kilpatrick, S. D., & Mooney, C. N. (2003). Narcissists as "victims": The role of narcissism in the perception of transgressions. *Personality and Social Psychology Bulletin, 29(7)*, 885–893. https://doi.org/10.1177/0146167203029007007.

Mechanic, K. L., & Barry, C. T. (2015). Adolescent grandiose and vulnerable narcissism: Associations with perceived parenting practices. *Journal of Child Family Studies, 24(5)*, 1510–1518. https://doi.org/10.1007/s10826-014-9956-x.

Miller, J. D., & Campbell, W. K. (2008). Comparing clinical and social-personality conceptualizations of narcissism. *Journal of Personality, 76(3)*, 449–476. https://doi.org/10.1111/j.1467-6494.2008.00492.x.

Miller, J. D., Dir, A., Gentile, B. et al. (2010). Searching for a vulnerable dark triad: Comparing Factor 2 psychopathy, vulnerable narcissism, and borderline personality disorder. *Journal of Personality, 78(5)*, 1529–1564. https://doi.org/10.1111/j.1467-6494.2010.00660.x.

Miller, J. D., Gaughan, E. T., Maples, J., & Price, J. A. (2011). Comparison of agreeableness scores from the Big Five inventor and the NEO

PI-R: Consequences for the study of narcissism and psychopathy. *Assessment, 18(3)*, 335–339. https://doi.org/10.1177/1073191111411671.

Miller, J. D., Lynam, D. R., & Campbell, W. K. (2016). Measures of narcissism and their relations to *DSM-5* pathological traits: A critical reappraisal. *Assessment, 23(1)*, 3–9. https://doi.org/10.1177/1073191114522909.

Miller, J. D., Lynam, D. R., Hyatt, C. S., & Campbell, W. K. (2017). Controversies in narcissism. *Annual Review of Clinical Psychology, 13*, 291–315. https://doi.org/10.1146/annurev-clinpsy-032816-045244.

Miller, J. D., Lynam, D. R., Vize, C. et al. (2018). Vulnerable narcissism is (mostly) a disorder of neuroticism. *Journal of Personality, 86(2)*, 186–199. https://doi.org/10.1111/jopy.12303.

Monell, E., Högdahl, L., Mantilla, E. F., & Birgegård, A. (2015). Emotion dysregulation, self-image, and eating disorder symptoms in university women. *Journal of Eating Disorders, 3(44)*, 1–11. https://doi.org/10.1186/s40337-015-0083-x.

Morf, C. C., & Rhodewalt, F. (2001). Unraveling the paradoxes of narcissism: A dynamic self-regulatory processing model. *Psychological Inquiry, 12(4)*, 177–196. https://doi.org/10.1207/S15327965PLI1204_1.

Morf, C. C., Weir, C., & Davidov, M. (2000). Narcissism and intrinsic motivation: The role of goal congruence. *Journal of Experimental Social Psychology, 36(4)*, 424–438. https://doi.org/10.1006/jesp.1999.1421.

Mountford, V., Corstorphine, E., Tomlinson, S., & Waller, G. (2007). Development of a measure to assess invalidating childhood environments in the eating disorders. *Eating Behavior, 8(1)*, 48–58. https://doi.org/10.1016/j.eatbeh.2006.01.003.

Nettle, D. (2005). An evolutionary approach to the extraversion continuum. *Evolution and Human Behavior, 26(4)*, 363–373. https://doi.org/10.1016/j.evolhumbehav.2004.12.004.

Nevicka, B. (2018). Narcissism and leadership: A perfect match? In A. D. Hermann, A. B. Brunell, & J. D. Foster (Eds.), *The handbook of trait narcissism: Key advances, research methods, and controversies* (pp. 399–407). New York: Springer. https://doi.org/10.1007/978-3-319-92171-6.

Nevicka, B., Baas, M., & Ten Velden, F. S. (2016). The bright side of threatened narcissism: Improved performance following ego threat. *Journal of Personality, 84(6)*, 809–823. https://doi.org/10.1111/jopy.12223.

Nevicka, B., De Hoogh, A. H. B., Van Vianen, A. E. M., Beersma, B., & McIlwain, D. (2011). All I need is a stage to shine: Narcissists' leader emergence and performance. *The Leadership Quarterly, 22(5)*, 910–925. https://doi.org/10.1016/j.leaqua.2011.07.011.

Nevicka, B., De Hoogh, A. H. B., Van Vianen, A. E. M., & Ten Velden, F. S. (2013). Uncertainty enhances the preference for narcissistic leaders. *European Journal of Social Psychology, 43(5)*, 370–380. https://doi.org/10.1002/ejsp.1943.

Nevicka, B., Van Vianen, A. E. M., De Hoogh, A. H. B., & Voorn, B. C. M. (2018). Narcissistic leaders: An asset or a liability? Leader visibility, follower responses, and group-level absenteeism. *Journal of Applied Psychology, 103 (7)*, 703–723. https://doi.org/10.1037/apl0000298.

Nevicka, B., Velden, F. S. T., De Hoogh, A. H. B., & Van Vianen, A. E. M. (2011). Reality at odds with perceptions: Narcissistic leaders and group performance. *Psychological Science, 22(10)*, 1259–1264. https://doi.org/10.1177/0956797611417259.

O'Boyle, E. H., Forsyth, D. R., Banks, G. C., & McDaniel, M. A. (2011). A meta-analysis of the Dark Triad and work behavior: A social exchange perspective. *Journal of Applied Psychology, 97(3)*, 557–579. https://doi.org/10.1037/a0025679.

O'Reilly, C. A., & Hall, N. (2021). Grandiose narcissists and decision making: Impulsive, overconfident, and skeptical of experts–but in doubt. *Personality and Individual Differences, 168(110280),* 1–11. https://doi.org/10.1016/j.paid.2020.110280.

Ou, A. Y., Tsui, A. S., Kinicki, A. et al. (2014). Humble chief executive officers' connections to top management team integration and middle managers' responses. *Administrative Science Quarterly, 59(1)*, 34–72. https://doi.org/10.1177/0001839213520131.

Overall, N. C., & Sibley, C. G. (2008). When accommodation matters: Situational dependency within daily interactions with romantic partners. *Journal of Experimental Social Psychology, 44(1)*, 95–104. https://doi.org/10.1016/j.jesp.2007.02.005.

Owens, B. P., Wallace, A. S., & Waldman, D. A. (2015). Leader narcissism and follower outcomes: The counterbalancing effect of leader humility. *Journal of Applied Psychology, 100(4)*, 1203–1213. https://doi.org/10.1037/a0038698.

Park, S. W., & Colvin, C. R. (2015). Narcissism and other-derogation in the absence of ego threat. *Journal of Personality, 83(3)*, 334–345. https://doi.org/10.1111/jopy.12107.

Paulhus, D. L. (1998). Interpersonal and intrapsychic adaptiveness of trait self-enhancement: A mixed blessing? *Journal of Personality and Social Psychology, 74(5)*, 1197–1208. https://doi.org/10.1037/0022-3514.74.5.1197.

Paulhus, D. L., & Williams, K. M. (2002). The dark triad of personality: Narcissism, Machiavellianism, and psychopathy. *Journal of Research in Personality, 36(6)*, 556–563. https://doi.org/10.1016/S0092-6566(02)00505-6.

Penney, L. M., & Spector, P. E. (2002). Narcissism and counterproductive work behavior: Do bigger egos mean bigger problems? *International Journal of Selection and Assessment, 10(1–2)*, 126–134. https://doi.org/10.1111/1468-2389.00199.

Peterson, J. L., & DeHart, T. (2014). In defense of self-love: An observational study on narcissists' negative behavior during romantic relationships conflict. *Self & Identity, 13(4)*, 477–490. https://doi.org/10.1080/15298868.2013.868368.

Philipson, I. (1985). Gender and narcissism. *Psychology of Women Quarterly, 9 (2)*, 213–228.

Pilch, I. (2020). As cold as a fish? Relationships between the Dark Triad personality traits and affective experience during the day: A day reconstruction study. *PLoS ONE, 15(2)*, 1–22, e0229625. https://doi.org/10.1371/journal.pone.0229625.

Pincus, A. L., & Lukowitsky, M. R. (2010). Pathological narcissism and narcissistic personality disorder. *Annual Review of Clinical Psychology, 6*, 421–446. https://doi.org/10.1146/annurev.clinpsy.121208.131215.

Pincus, A. L., Pimentel, C. A., Cain, N. M. et al. (2009). Initial construction and validation of the Pathological Narcissism Inventory. *Psychological Assessment, 21(3)*, 365–379. https://doi.org/10.1037/a0016530.

Porath, C. L., & Erez, A. (2007). Does rudeness really matter? The effects of rudeness on task performance and helpfulness. *Academy of Management Journal, 50(5)*, 1181–1197. https://doi.org/10.2307/20159919.

Prins, K. S., Buunk, B. P., & VanYperen, N. W. (1993). Equity, normative disapproval and extramarital relationships. *Journal of Social and Personal Relationships, 10(1)*, 39–53. http://dx-doi-org.proxy.lib.ohio-state.edu/10.1177/0265407593101003.

Raskin, R. N., & Hall, C. S. (1979). A narcissistic personality inventory. *Psychological Reports, 45(2)*, 590. https://doi.org/10.2466/pr0.1979.45.2.590.

Raskin, R., & Terry, H. (1988). A principal-components analysis of the narcissistic personality inventory and further evidence of its construct validity. *Journal of Personality and Social Psychology, 54(5)*, 890–902. https://doi.org/10.1037/0022-3514.54.5.890.

Rauthmann, J. F., & Will, T. (2011). Proposing a multidimensional Machiavellianism conceptualization. *Social Behavior and Personality: An International Journal, 39(3)*, 391–403. https://doi.org/10.2224/sbp.2011.39.3.391.

Rentzsch, K., & Gebauer, J. E. (2019). On the popularity of agentic and communal narcissists: The tit-for-tat hypothesis. *Personality and Social Psychology Bulletin, 45(9)*, 1365–1377. https://doi.org/10.1177/0146167218824359.

Resick, C. J., Whitman, D. S., Weingarden, S. M., & Hiller, N. J. (2009). The bright-side and the dark-side of CEO personality: Examining core self-evaluations, narcissism, transformational leadership, and strategic influence. *Journal of Applied Psychology, 94(6)*, 1365–1381. https://doi.org/10.1037/a0016238.

Robbins, S. P., & Judge, T. A. (2011). *Organizational behavior, 14th Ed.*, Indianapolis, IN: Pearson.

Rogoza, R., Cieciuch, J., Strus, W., & Baran, T. (2019). Seeking a common framework for research on narcissism: An attempt to integrate the different faces of narcissism within the circumplex of personality metatraits. *European Journal of Personality, 33(4)*, 437–455. https://doi.org/10.1002/per.2206.

Rogoza, R., & Fatfouta, R. (2019). Normal and pathological communal narcissism in relation to personality traits and values. *Personality and Individual Differences, 140*, 76–81. https://doi.org/10.1016/j.paid.2018.03.039.

Rohmann, E., Neumann, E., Herner, M. J., & Bierhoff, H. W. (2012). Grandiose and vulnerable narcissism: Self-construal, attachment, and love in romantic relationships. *European Psychologist, 17(4)*, 279–290. https://doi.org/10.1027/1016-9040/a000100.

Rosenthal, S. A., & Pittinsky, T. L. (2006). Narcissistic leadership. *The Leadership Quarterly, 17(6)*, 617–633. https://doi.org/10.1016/j.leaqua.2006.10.005.

Rudman, L. A. (1998). Self-promotion as a risk factor for women: The costs and benefits of counterstereotypical impression management. *Journal of Personality and Social Psychology, 74(3)*, 629–645. https://doi.org/10.1037/0022-3514.74.3.629.

Rusbult, C. E. (1980). Commitment and satisfaction in romantic associations: A test of the investment model. *Journal of Experimental Social Psychology, 16(2)*, 172–186. https://doi.org/10.1016/0022-1031(80)90007-4.

Rusbult, C. E. (1983). A longitudinal test of the investment model: The development (and deterioration) of satisfaction and commitment in heterosexual involvements. *Journal of Personality and Social Psychology, 45(1)*, 101–117. https://doi.org/10.1037/0022-3514.45.1.101.

Rusbult, C. E., Johnson, D. J., & Morrow, G. D. (1986). Impact of couple patterns of problem solving distress and nondistress in dating relationships. *Journal of Personality and Social Psychology, 50(4)*, 744–753. https://doi.org/10.1037/0022-3514.50.4.744.

Rusbult, C. E., & Zembrodt, I. M. (1983). Responses to dissatisfaction in romantic involvements: A multidimensional scaling analysis. *Journal of*

Experimental Social Psychology 19(3), 274–293. https://doi.org/10.1016/0022-1031(83)90042-2.

Russ, E., Shedler, J., Bradley, R., & Westen, D. (2008). Refining the construct of narcissistic personality disorder: Diagnostic criteria and subtypes. *The American Journal of Psychiatry, 165(11)*, 1473–1481. https://doi.org/10.1176/appi.ajp.2008.07030376.

Salekin, R. T., & Lynam, D. R. (Eds.) (2010). *Handbook of child and adolescent psychopathy*. New York, NY: Guilford.

Samuel, D. B., & Widiger, T. A. (2008). Convergence of narcissism measures from the perspective of general personality functioning. *Assessment, 15(3)*, 364–374. https://doi.org/10.1177/1073191108314278.

Schilpzand, P., De Pater, I., & Erez, A. (2016). Workplace incivility: A review of the literature and agenda for future research. *Journal of Organizational Behavior, 37*, S57–S88. https://doi.org/10.1002/job.1976.

Schmid, E. A., Knipfer, K., & Peus, C. V. (2021). Narcissistic leaders–promise or peril? The patterns of narcissistic leaders' behaviors and their relation to team performance. *Frontiers in Psychology, 12(660452)*, 1–18. https://doi.org/10.3389/fpsyg.2021.660452.

Schmitt, D. P., Alcalay, L., Allik, J. et al. (2017). Narcissism and the strategic pursuit of short-term mating: Universal links across 11 world regions of the international sexuality description project-2. *Psihologijske Teme, 26(1)*, 89–137. https://doi.org/10.31820/pt.26.1.5.

Schoenleber, M., Roche, M. J., Wetzel, E., Pincus, A. L., & Roberts, B. W. (2015). Development of a brief version of the Pathological Narcissism Inventory. *Psychological Assessment, 27(4)*, 1520–1526. https://doi.org/10.1037/pas0000158.

Slater, P. (1974). *Earthwalk*. Milwaukee, WI: Anchor Press.

Smith-Jentsch, K. A., Sullivan, S. E., & Ford, R. C. (2019). Toxic mentors and how to deal with them. *Organizational Dynamics, 48(4)*, 1–8. https://doi-org.proxy.lib.ohio-state.edu/10.1016/j.orgdyn.2018.08.002.

Sprecher, S., Schmeeckle, M., & Felmlee, D. (2006). The Principle of Least Interest: Inequality in Emotional Involvement in Romantic Relationships. *Journal of Family Issues, 27(9)*, 1255–1280. https://doi.org/10.1177/0192513X06289215.

Stone, B. M., & Bartholomay, E. M. (2022). A two-factor structure of the hypersensitive narcissism scale describes gender-dependent manifestations of covert narcissism. *Current Psychology: A Journal for Diverse Perspectives on Diverse Psychological Issues, 41(9)*, 6051–6062. https://doi.org/10.1007/s12144-020-01088-2.

Strus, W., & Cieciuch, J. (2017). Towards a synthesis of personality, temperament, motivation, emotion, and mental health models within the Circumplex of Personality Metatraits. *Journal of Research in Personality, 66*, 70–95. https://doi.org/10.1016/j.jrp.2016.12.002.

Stucke, T. S. (2003). Who's to blame? Narcissism and self-serving attributions following feedback. *European Journal of Personality, 17(6)*, 465–478. https://doi.org/10.1002/per.497.

Tanchotsrinon, P., Maneesri, K., & Campbell, W. K. (2007). Narcissism and romantic attraction: Evidence from a collectivistic culture. *Journal of Research in Personality, 41(3)*, 723–730. https://doi.org/10.1016/j.jrp.2006.08.004.

Thomas, K. M., Wright, A. G. C., Lukowitsky, M. R., Donnellan, M. B., & Hopwood, C. J. (2012). Evidence for the criterion validity and clinical utility of the pathological narcissism inventory. *Assessment, 19(2)*, 135–145. https://doi.org/10.1177/1073191112436664.

Thomaes, S., Brummelman, E., & Sedikides, C. (2018). Narcissism: A social-developmental perspective. In V. Zeigler-Hill & T. K. Shackelford (Eds.), *The SAGE handbook of personality and individual differences: Applications of personality and individual differences* (pp. 377–396). Washington, DC: Sage Reference. https://doi-org.proxy.lib.ohio-state.edu/10.4135/9781526451248.n16.

Tortoriello, G. K., Hart, W., Richardson, K., & Tullett, A. M. (2017). Do narcissists try to make romantic partners jealous on purpose? An examination of the motives for deliberate jealousy-induction among subtypes of narcissism. *Personality and Individual Differences, 114*, 10–15. https://doi.org/10.1016/j.paid.2017.03.052.

Trull, T. J., & McCrae, R. R. (2002). A five-factor perspective on personality disorder research. In P. T. Costa, Jr. & T. A. Widiger (Eds.), *Personality disorders and the five-factor model of personality* (pp. 45–57). Washington, DC: American Psychological Association. https://doi.org/10.1037/10423-004.

Trzesniewski, K. H., Donnellan, M. B., & Robins, R. W. (2008). Is "generation me" really more narcissistic than previous generations? *Journal of Personality, 76(4)*, 903–918. https://doi.org/10.1111/j.1467-6494.2008.00508.x.

Tschanz, B. T., Morf, C. C., & Turner, C. W. (1998). Gender differences in the structure of narcissism: A multi-sample analysis of the Narcissistic Personality Inventory. *Sex Roles: A Journal of Research, 38(9–10)*, 863–870. https://doi.org/10.1023/A:1018833400411.

Turner, I. N., & Webster, G. D. (2018). Narcissism and dark personality traits. In A. D. Hermann, A. B. Brunell, & J. D. Foster (Eds.), *The handbook of trait narcissism: Key advances, research methods, and controversies* (pp. 205–212). New York, NY: Springer. https://doi.org/10.1007/978-3-319-92171-6.

Twenge, J. M., Konrath, S., Foster, J. D., Campbell, W. K., & Bushman, B. J. (2008a). Egos inflating over time: A cross-temporal meta-analysis of the Narcissistic Personality Inventory. *Journal of Personality, 76(4)*, 875–902. https://doi-org.proxy.lib.ohio-state.edu/10.1111/j.1467-6494.2008.00507.x.

Twenge, J. M., Konrath, S., Foster, J. D., Campbell, W. K., & Bushman, B. J. (2008b). Further evidence of an increase in narcissism among college students. *Journal of Personality, 76(4)*, 919–928. https://doi-org.proxy.lib.ohio-state.edu/10.1111/j.1467-6494.2008.00509.x.

Van Dyne, L., Vandewalle, D., Kostoya, T., Latham, M. E., & Cummings, L. L. (2000). Collectivism propensity to trust, and self-esteem as predictors of organizational citizenship in a non-work setting. *Journal of Organizational Behavior, 21(1)*, 3–23. https://doi.org/10.1002/(SICI)1099-1379(200002)21:1<3::AID-JOB47>3.0.CO;2-6.

van Schie, C. C., Jarman, H. L., Huxley, E., & Grenyer, B. F. S. (2020). Narcissistic traits in young people: Understanding the role of parenting and maltreatment. *Borderline Personality Disorder and Emotion Dysregulation*, *7*, 10, 1–11. https://doi.org/10.1186/s40479-020-00125-7.

Veselka, L., Giammarco, E. A., & Vernon, P. A. (2014). The Dark Triad and the seven deadly sins. *Personality and Individual Differences*, *67*, 75–80. https://doi.org/10.1016/j.paid.2014.01.055.

Visser, B. A. (2018). Narcissism and the Big Five/HEXACO models of personality. In A. D. Hermann, A. B. Brunell, & J. D. Foster (Eds.), *The handbook of trait narcissism: Key advances, research methods, and controversies* (pp. 205–212). New York: Springer. https://doi.org/10.1007/978-3-319-92171-6.

Vonk, J., Zeigler-Hill, V., Mayhew, P., & Mercer, S. (2013). Mirror, mirror on the wall, which form of narcissist knows self and others best of all? *Personality and Individual Differences*, *54(3)*, 396–401. https://doi.org/10.1016/j.paid.2012.10.010.

Vrabel, J. K., Zeigler-Hill, V., Lehtman, M., & Hernandez, K. (2020). Narcissism and perceived power in romantic relationships. *Journal of Social and Personal Relationships*, *37(1)*, 124–142. https://doi-org.proxy.lib.ohio-state.edu/10.1177/0265407519858685.

Wallace, H. M. (2011). Narcissistic self-enhancement. In W. K. Campbell & J. D. Miller (Eds.), *The handbook of narcissism and narcissistic personality disorder: Theoretical approaches, empirical findings, and treatments* (pp. 309–318). Hoboken, NJ: John Wiley & Sons.

Wallace, H. M., Ready, C. B., & Weitenhagen, E. (2009). Narcissism and task persistence. *Self and Identity*, *8(1)*, 78–93. https://doi.org/10.1080/15298860802194346.

Wallace, H. M., Scheiner, B. R. M., & Grotzinger, A. (2016). Grandiose narcissism predicts willingness to behave badly, without proportional tolerance for others' bad behavior. *Current Psychology, 35(2)*, 234–243. https://doi.org/10.1007/s12144-016-9410-x.

Waller, W. W. (1938). *The family: A dynamic interpretation*. Fort Worth, TX: The Dryden Press.

Watson, P. J., Taylor, D., & Morris, R. J. (1987). Narcissism, sex roles, and self-functioning. *Sex Roles: A Journal of Research, 16(7–8)*, 335–350. https://doi.org/10.1007/BF00289546.

Watts, A. L., Lileinfeld, S. O., Smith, S. F. et al. (2013). The double-edged sword of grandiose narcissism: Implications for successful and unsuccessful leadership among U.S. Presidents. *Psychological Science, 24(12)*, 2379–2389. https://doi.org/10.1177/0956797613491970.

Weidmann, R., Chopik, W. J., Ackerman, R. A. et al. (2023). Age and gender differences in narcissism: A comprehensive study across eight measures and over 250,000 participants. *Journal of Personality and Social Psychology, 124 (6)*, 1277–1298. https://doi-org.proxy.lib.ohio-state.edu/10.1037/pspp0000463.

Wetzel, E., Grijalva, E., Robins, R. W., & Roberts, B. W. (2020). You're still so vain: Changes in narcissism from young adulthood to middle age. *Journal of Personality and Social Psychology, 119(2)*, 479–496. https://doi.org/10.1037/pspp0000266.

Wetzel, E., & Robins, R. W. (2016). Are parenting practices associated with the development of narcissism? Findings from a longitudinal study of Mexican-origin youth. *Journal of Research in Personality, 63*, 84–94. https://doi.org/10.1016/j.jrp.2016.05.005.

Wilson, M. S., & Sibley, C. G. (2011). "Narcissism creep?": Evidence for age-related differences in narcissism in the New Zealand general population. *New Zealand Journal of Psychology, 40(3)*, 89–95.

Winner, N. A., & Nicholson, B. C. (2018). Overparenting and narcissism in young adults: The mediating role of psychological control. *Journal of Child and Family Studies, 27(11)*, 3650–3657. https://doi.org/10.1007/s10826-018-1176-3.

Wink, P. (1991). Two faces of narcissism. *Journal of Personality and Social Psychology, 61(4)*, 590–597. https://doi.org/10.1037/0022-3514.61.4.590.

Wink, P. (1992). Three narcissism scales for the California Q-set. *Journal of Personality Assessment, 58(1)*, 51–66. https://doi.org/10.1207/s15327752jpa5801_5.

Wirtz, N., & Rigotti, T. (2020). When grandiose meets vulnerable: Narcissism and well-being in the organizational context. *European Journal of Work and Organizational Psychology, 29(4)*, 556–569. https://doi.org/10.1080/1359432X.2020.1731474.

Wood, W., & Eagly, A. H. (2012). Biosocial construction of sex differences and similarities in behavior. In J. M., Olson & M. P. Zanna (Eds.), *Advances in experimental social psychology* (Vol. 46. pp. 55–123). Cambridge, MA: Elsevier. https://doi.org/10.1016/B978-0-12-394281-4.00002-7.

Ye, S., Lam, Z. K. W., Ma, Z., & Ng, T. K. (2016). Differential relations of narcissism and self-esteem to romantic relationships: The mediating role of perception discrepancy. *Asian Journal of Social Psychology, 19(4)*, 374–384. https://doi.org/10.1111/ajsp.12160.

Zerach, G. (2014). The associations between pathological narcissism, alexithymia and disordered eating attitudes among participants of pro-anorexic online communities. *Eating and Weight Disorders, 19(3)*, 337–345. https://doi.org/10.1007/s40519-013-0096-x.

Zitek, E. M., & Jordan, A. H. (2016). Narcissism predicts support for hierarchy (at least when narcissists think they can rise to the top). *Social Psychological and Personality Science, 7(7)*, 707–716. https://doi.org/10.1177/1948550616649241.

Cambridge Elements

Applied Social Psychology

Susan Clayton
College of Wooster, Ohio
Susan Clayton is a social psychologist at the College of Wooster in Wooster, Ohio. Her research focuses on the human relationship with nature, how it is socially constructed, and how it can be utilized to promote environmental concern.

Editorial Board

About the Series

Many social psychologists have used their research to understand and address pressing social issues, from poverty and prejudice to work and health. Each Element in this series reviews a particular area of applied social psychology. Elements will also discuss applications of the research findings and describe directions for future study.

Cambridge Elements

Applied Social Psychology

Elements in the Series

The Psychology of Climate Change Adaptation
Anne van Valkengoed and Linda Steg

Undoing the Gender Binary
Charlotte Chucky Tate, Ella Ben Hagai, and Faye J. Crosby

Selves as Solutions to Social Inequalities: Why Engaging the Full Complexity of Social Identities is Critical to Addressing Disparities
Tiffany N. Brannon, Peter H. Fisher, and Abigail J. Greydanus

Identity Development During STEM Integration for Underrepresented Minority Students
Sophie L. Kuchynka, Alexander E. Gates, and Luis M. Rivera

The Psychology of Effective Activism
Robyn Gulliver, Susilo Wibisono, Kelly S. Fielding, and Winnifred R. Louis

Learning from Video Games (and Everything Else): The General Learning Model
Douglas A. Gentile and J. Ronald Gentile

Climate Change and Human Behavior: Impacts of a Rapidly Changing Climate on Human Aggression and Violence
Andreas Miles-Novelo and Craig A. Anderson

Behavioral Insights for Public Policy: Contextualizing Our Science
Crystal C. Hall and Ines Jurcevic

Entrapment, Escape, and Elevation from Relationship Violence
Wind Goodfriend and Pamela Lassiter Simcock

Two or More: A Comparative Analysis of Multiracial and Multicultural Research
Analia F. Albuja, Alexandria West, and Sarah E. Gaither

Hate Speech
Janet B. Ruscher

Understanding and Coping in Social Relationships with Narcissists
Amy B. Brunell

A full series listing is available at: www.cambridge.org/EASP

www.ingramcontent.com/pod-product-compliance
Ingram Content Group UK Ltd.
Pitfield, Milton Keynes, MK11 3LW, UK
UKHW031541100125
453394UK00008B/80